WHAT IS GOD DOING IN ISRAEL?

Also by Julia Fisher:

Meet Me at the Olive Tree
Israel's New Disciples
Israel, the Mystery of Peace
Future for Israel?

What is God Doing in Israel?

When Jews and Palestinians meet Jesus

Julia Fisher

MONARCH
BOOKS
Oxford, UK, and Grand Rapids, USA

Published by Monarch Books
an imprint of
Lion Hudson plc
Wilkinson House, Jordan Hill Road,
Oxford OX2 8DR, England
Email: monarch@lionhudson.com
www.lionhudson.com/monarch

ISBN 978 0 85721 685 4
e-ISBN 978 0 85721 686 1

First edition 2016

Acknowledgments
Unless otherwise stated, Scripture quotations are taken from the Holy Bible, New
International Version Anglicised. Copyright © 1979, 1984, 2011 Biblica, formerly
International Bible Society. Used by permission of Hodder & Stoughton Ltd, an
Hachette UK company. All rights reserved. "NIV" is a registered trademark of
Biblica. UK trademark number 1448790.
Scripture quotations marked "NLT" are taken from the Holy Bible, New Living
Translation, copyright © 1996, 2004, 2007 by Tyndale House Foundation. Used by
permission of Tyndale House Publishers, Inc., Carol Stream, Illinois 60188. All rights
reserved.
Extract pp. 235–236 taken from "Six-Day War" in *Encyclopaedia Britannica*
www.britannica.com/event/Six-Day-War. Used by permission of *Encyclopaedia
Britannica Online*.
Extract pp. 236–37 taken from "Moqattam's hidden treasure: Saint Samaan Church"
by Abdel-Rahman Shereif, 14 February 2013. Used by permission of *Daily News Egypt*.

A catalogue record for this book is available from the British Library

Printed and bound in the UK, January 2016, LH26

Contents

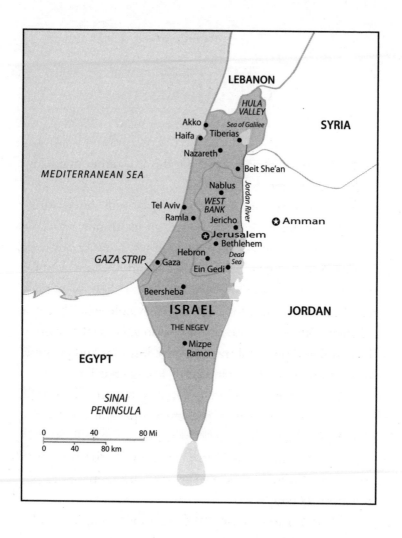

LEBANON

HULA VALLEY

SYRIA

Akko
Sea of Galilee
Haifa • Tiberias

Nazareth

MEDITERRANEAN SEA

Beit She'an

Nablus

WEST BANK

Tel Aviv •
Ramla •

Jericho

Jordan River

Amman

Jerusalem
Bethlehem

GAZA STRIP

Hebron
Gaza

Dead Sea

Ein Gedi

Beersheba

ISRAEL

JORDAN

THE NEGEV

EGYPT

• Mizpe Ramon

SINAI PENINSULA

| 0 | 40 | 80 Mi |
| 0 | 40 | 80 km |

Introduction

If you are already thinking this is a rather audacious title, let me explain!

In reading this book you will be entering another world; a world of persecution, trouble, conflict, and fear. You will be experiencing everyday life for Jews and Palestinians who believe in Jesus and who live in Israel, the West Bank, and the Middle East. Their stories are challenging because they are about people who, because of their faith, have variously been disowned by their family, have suffered personal tragedy, have lost jobs and personal reputation, or are living in fear of losing their life.

At the same time, these are stories that are full of hope and life and excitement. The same people will tell you that their faith in Jesus, Yeshua, is more important to them than anything else and that if they have to die for what they believe and who they believe in, they are prepared to pay the ultimate cost.

So who better to ask, "What is God doing in Israel?" than the people who believe in Him who live there? After all, they are the ones who are living out their faith there.

In this book you will meet Muslims who have become believers in Jesus, some of whom are now suffering greatly as a result as they have lost not only their jobs and reputations, but they have also been disowned by their families and in some cases are living in fear of their lives. You will read about Jewish people who have immigrated to Israel from the four corners of the world, including India, Russia, Morocco, and America. What was it that persuaded them to leave the land where their families had lived for generations and move to another country where life would be hard? And what about those evangelical Palestinian Christians living as a tiny minority group among the much larger majority Muslim Palestinian population? These are people who often feel ignored by Christians in the West yet, as you will discover, they have a strong sense of calling to live out their God-given destiny in Israel and the West Bank today. Surprisingly, perhaps, you will read of Arab Christians who have come to Israel from neighbouring Arab countries. As for Jewish believers who are emissaries to the Muslim world, yes, even this is going on! In short, when asking about what God is doing in Israel and the Middle East today you find there are some very unexpected things happening, especially when placed against the backdrop of the turmoil that is the Middle East.

And by being prepared to open yourself to the diverse stories of these people, you will, I hope, gain an insight into what God is doing in Israel and the Palestinian areas of the West Bank today. I am sure that all Christians would agree that the Bible has much to say prophetically about the land of Israel and its people. However, when interpreting prophecy, it seems there are many opinions! Perhaps the stories in this book will reveal some hitherto hidden threads that will help in your understanding.

While the people whose stories have been included in this book do not all share the same political and theological views, it is not the intention of this book to engage in political or theological debate. Rather it is simply to present another view, a view that can only be gained by spending time with people and listening to their stories told humbly and honestly, from the heart. Listening to these people sharing their stories and explaining their understanding of what God is doing today in light of their understanding of Scripture is, as you will read, revealing.

For the past twenty years I have been privileged, as a journalist, to be able to visit Israel and the West Bank regularly to research and record the stories of believers in Jesus who live there, both Messianic Jews and Palestinian Christians. Because of the personal cost to them of living in the region, the question, "What do you believe God is doing in Israel and the wider Middle East today?" seems the most pertinent question to ask. Why else would they stay? Perhaps because of the personal cost involved, I have not met any half-hearted believers in Jesus living in the region. This is an area of the world where what you believe defines who you are and where you come from. To switch belief from being either an observant Jew or a religious Muslim to become a believer in Yeshua, Jesus, is therefore a decision that is not taken lightly, as you will discover.

All the people you will read about in this book are people I have spent considerable time with. Many I have met several times over the years as I have followed their stories. Others are new contacts and represent stories that are emerging. I thank them all for being willing to share their lives and be included in this book so that you can engage with them and, more importantly, with what God is doing in Israel and the rest of the world in these days in which we live.

Julia Fisher
July 2015

CHAPTER 1

David and Leah Ortiz in America

On 20 March 2008, fifteen-year-old Ami Ortiz was almost killed by a bomb that was left in a Purim parcel[1] outside the family's apartment in the city of Ariel in Israel. For months afterwards I read with both anguish and interest the news of his recovery. The reports, regularly written by his mother Leah, reflected the shock and pain felt by the family as well as the ability to forgive the man who had committed this atrocity. The Ortiz family displayed great dignity, integrity, and faith.

This is the story of a family who, when they moved to Ariel,[2] experienced a level of harassment and persecution from Jewish people living in their neighbourhood who were prepared to resort to violence and intimidation because they found the faith of the Ortiz family unacceptable and threatening to their Jewish way of life. The name and person of Yeshua was so abhorrent to many of the Orthodox and secular Jews who lived in Ariel that they were determined to hound this "missionary" family out of town.

I first met David and Leah in Beer Sheva where I went to interview members of Jews for Jesus who were there conducting one of their evangelistic campaigns. Having spoken to many of the team, I was asked if I would like to meet the team's chaplains.

"Who are they?" I enquired.

"David and Leah Ortiz," came the reply. "David is resting as he is recovering from major surgery, but let me go and ask them if they would like to talk to you."

Having heard so much about David and Leah Ortiz and having followed Ami's story, I was particularly keen to meet them and delighted when the message came that they would be free in an hour.

My first impression was how self-effacing they are and genuinely interested in other people. We only had a short time together, but their talk was of how pleased they were to be able to work alongside the Jews for Jesus team and support them.

They invited me to visit them on my next visit. "Come to our home in Ariel," they said.

A few months later, climbing the stairs to their apartment on the third floor, knowing what had happened to Ami on that fateful day in March 2008 and how much damage their apartment had suffered as a result of the bomb, I wondered what to expect.

David and Leah showed me what remained of their dining room table after the bomb had exploded: it was no longer a table, more a frame surrounding a gaping hole. "The walls were riddled with shrapnel, there were holes in the ceiling above where the bomb exploded, and all the windows were shattered," they told me. Everything in the apartment had been destroyed by the blast. But David and Leah were convinced that God wanted them to stay in Ariel and repair their home and carry on with their work.

This is their story, and it gives an insight into what God is doing in Israel at this time. I spoke first to David, who is originally from Puerto Rico, to find out how he had developed a yearning to live in Israel.

David's story ...

Although I was born in Puerto Rico, when I was six months old my parents moved to New York where I was raised. We were five children; later on we were six because my parents adopted a six-month-old cousin whose mother was murdered. In the house we spoke Spanish, outside we spoke English, and later on I spoke Yiddish with my friends.

I found New York fascinating because there were people there from many nations, including a large Jewish population, many of whom had come from Europe having survived the Holocaust. Little did I realize then how influential these people would be in shaping the future destiny of my life.

When I was seven my father began working for a company that imported and exported a variety of goods. The owners of the company were Orthodox Jewish Holocaust survivors. When they came to the United States they started a wholesale clothing business and sold to many Jewish people all over the world. There I met Jews from Iran, Jews from Cuba,

Jews from Argentina, Jews from Greece and Slovakia, Jews from Europe; in fact, Jews from every corner of the world. There I learned about the world and heard about places hitherto unknown to me.

My father started bringing books home about the Holocaust. For me this was an education. I was reading about events in Europe that I had previously never heard about. When I reached the age of twelve, during the school holidays my father took me to work with him. I was fascinated to meet Jewish people from so many different countries, and as I listened to their many and varied stories, I started to understand a little of their long history, which in turn increased my interest in them as a people group.

Each day, later in the afternoon when the store was quiet, I watched as the owners gathered for prayer. They would respectfully open their Jewish prayer books and the Talmud[3] and other Jewish writings. Although I was not Jewish myself, they soon realized I was interested in what they were doing. They started to teach me about Jewish history and they introduced me to some Jewish writings and literature. I found it fascinating, and as I grew older I started to work there in my vacations.

When I was fourteen years old, something happened that shook my world – my parents decided to move back to Puerto Rico and build a house there. In Puerto Rico they and my sisters became believers in Jesus but I did not want to embrace the faith of my family. They talked about Jesus from morning to night and I found it really disturbing, like nails scraping against glass. So, a few years later, when I was sixteen, I left my family in Puerto Rico and returned to New York. For a short time I lived with some relatives while I looked for a room to rent and happily resumed working for the Jewish company.

I was determined to make a success of my life in New York and so I studied to finish high school in the mornings and worked part time in the afternoons.

One day I arranged to meet a friend on a ferry boat. As I was waiting for him to arrive, a stranger came up to me and started talking about Jesus! He sounded just like my mother! As my friend hadn't arrived I decided to amuse myself and talk to this "Jesus" person for a while. I challenged him, "If you can show me in the Bible where it says Jesus is 'the way', I'll accept him right now."

"That's simple," he replied. Immediately I felt afraid. He opened his Bible and read to me, " 'Jesus said, I am the way and the truth and the life.' " I was shocked and realized I had no excuse before God now! When he asked me to pray the Sinner's Prayer,[4] I agreed, but just so I would have "fire insurance", as it were, to keep me out of hell. I could say to the Lord that I had prayed the prayer, and go on to live my life the way I wanted to. At that moment, my friend arrived and was interested to know who and what we were talking about. When I told him I was about to pray, he offered to join in!

Four months passed and I thought no more about the man on the ferry. Then, one night, I got into a violent argument with someone in which I picked up a knife and almost killed him. I actually felt something inside my arm pushing my arm forward. I was scared because I realized I had lost control of myself. Returning to my apartment I prayed, "Lord help me." Immediately I felt something warm on the top of my head and then I was quite literally flung from one side of the living room to the other. It was a large apartment and my flatmate watched as I "flew". Demons came out of me – I could feel them coming out of my back. After that, everything changed. My thought patterns changed and all the evil thoughts that had previously filled my head were gone.

The next day I went to work as usual and said to one of the Orthodox Jewish men, "Something happened to me yesterday and I have to tell you about it."

"What happened?" he said.

"I've become a Christian."

He said, "You've always been a Christian 'cos you're not a Muslim and you're not Jewish!"

I told him, "I was born a pagan but when I accepted Jesus as my Lord, I became a Christian. I also got filled with the Holy Spirit and the Lord spoke to me."

"How could this be?" he replied, "God only spoke to Moses; how come He spoke to you?"

So I tried to explain what had happened and how the demons had come out of me.

"David, we've known you from the age of seven. I'm looking into your eyes and I can see you're telling me the truth, but it's very hard to understand because we can never accept Jesus."

I had a strong desire to read the Bible and find out

more about Jesus. So on my way home from work one day I went to the Hebrew publishing company owned by the Hasidim[5] and asked for a New Testament. At that time I didn't appreciate the difference between the Old and New Testaments – I thought the New Testament was an updated version of the Old!

"I want to buy a New Testament," I said to the owner.

He said, "We don't have the New Testament."

I said, "Really?" and left the shop.

I walked a little way up the street and stopped. "Maybe I didn't say it right." So I turned round and went back to the shop. "Excuse me, do you have a New Testament?"

He said, "We don't have the New Testament."

I walked out. But the Lord told me, "Go back and ask again." I thought, maybe he didn't hear me.

So I went back. "Excuse me, but do you have the New Testament?"

His face got red and he shouted, "Get away from here. Old Testament yes, New Testament no! Get away from here." He was screaming at me and everybody in the shop turned round to look at me. "Go to 56 Second Avenue. Get away from here."

So I ran all the way to 56 Second Avenue, which was about seven blocks away. When I arrived I saw a big window filled with some pictures of rabbis. I thought to myself that these people would have the same problem with me as the Hasidic Jewish bookseller, but then I saw a small sign which read, "We have found Jesus the Messiah whom Moses spoke of."

I knocked on the door. A man answered. I asked him if he would sell me a New Testament. He said, "We can't sell you a New Testament but we can give you one for free."

I said, "For free? You mean no money at all?"

He said, "Yes, it's a gift."

I followed him upstairs and he gave me a New Testament. When I opened it and started to read I felt drunk. I started moving back and forth. I didn't understand what was happening to me. Apparently I had knocked on the door of a Jewish mission.

"You're getting drunk in the Holy Spirit," the man said to me. "Would you like to stay and have some dinner?"

I looked at him, "You don't know me and you're inviting me to dinner?" I didn't feel comfortable, and then I remembered I had a hole in my shoe!

At that moment another guy appeared called Gil who was an Eskimo, originally from Alaska. "Are you joining us for dinner?" he asked.

I said, "No."

He said, "Don't worry, I have a hole in my shoe too!" And he lifted up his foot and showed me the hole in his shoe.

I said, "How did you know I had a hole in my shoe?"

He said, "You're supposed to come to dinner."

So we went upstairs and had dinner.

Now my flatmates were involved in organized crime. They could make $15,000 in a matter of fifteen minutes selling drugs. So when I arrived home later that night and told them what had happened to me they looked uncomfortable. I could continue going in my new direction, they told me, but they would continue in theirs. Two weeks later, however, they told me to leave. "You have to go, you cannot talk about Jesus in this house – you will destroy the gang."

Not knowing where I would go, I started to pack my bags, but the day before I planned to leave, one of them came to talk to me. He told me he wanted to become a believer. Then, one by one, all my flatmates became believers! It was like a domino effect, and in a short time twenty people had become believers, and they are all still serving the Lord in ministry today.

So I continued with my work and also continued to visit the folk at the Jewish mission. They talked a lot about biblical prophecy. Chapter 31 of Jeremiah[6] was one of the chapters we discussed about how God would make a new covenant with the House of Israel. So when I went to work I mentioned this chapter in Jeremiah to the Orthodox Jews.

"David," they said, "we want to talk to you frankly. Don't mention Jesus." I had never seen them so agitated. "We will never accept him."

I went upstairs to the second floor and prayed, "Lord, this is pretty bad. These people are not going to make it to heaven because that covenant was with the Jewish people. It's a new covenant – what am I going to do?"

All of a sudden I felt a burden and heard the voice of God, like a man speaks to another, "Don't go to the Gentiles, but go to the lost sheep of the house of Israel." I started to laugh. To me that seemed so funny.

You don't send a Gentile Spanish-speaking Puerto Rican to these people – they won't listen to me! You send a Jew to the Jews. But then I remembered that in his letter to the Romans Paul had quoted from the prophet Hosea, "I will call them ' my people' who are not my people, and I will call her 'my loved one' who is not my loved one."[7]

I may not be Jewish, I realized, yet God counts me as one of His people because I believe in Jesus. Energized by this new revelation I started witnessing more to the Jewish people I was working with, and I could see they were curious, even jealous for what I had.

It was at this time I knew I had to go to Israel to live and work. I believed God was calling me. But how was it going to happen?

Later that night I was in my apartment thinking about how I would go to Israel when one of my flatmates, who was from India, came into my room, "I want to tell you something, David – you're lonely. You need a wife."

I said, "I'm not lonely."

"You're lonely," he insisted.

"Listen, I don't get lonely," and at that he left and closed the door.

I knelt down and cried out to the Lord, "I'm so lonely, what am I going to do? I guess he's right!" So I randomly opened the Bible and put my finger on a page which happened to be in the book of Psalms. I could not believe what I was reading,

> Your wife will be like a fruitful vine
> within your house.[8]

"This means I don't need to ask for a wife; I should pray for her! According to this, she's there already!" So I started praying, "Lord, get her ready for me, prepare her; get her really ready for me! And bring healing to my life so that when I meet her I will be ready too."

At this point, I turned to Leah who had been sitting quietly listening to her husband recount his early life. It struck me that Leah must have heard David's story many times yet she listened attentively to every word he said and smiled encouragement at him throughout, and even laughed at his jokes! It was clear that although they are from very different backgrounds, David and Leah have grown very close and, as you will read, they have dealt with many difficult situations over the years.

Leah takes up the story ...

> Surely goodness and love will follow me
> all the days of my life,
> and I will dwell in the house of the Lord
> for ever.[9]

When I was young in the faith, and in my twenties, I thought these words from Psalm 23 meant that only good and merciful things would happen to me throughout my life and I could look forward to a life of blessing in all of my circumstances. Now, having lived through and survived a diagnosis of multiple sclerosis for myself, a bomb explosion that critically wounded and scarred our youngest son, and an almost fatal mistake in my husband David's operation along with a cancer diagnosis, I understand the verse very differently. Not only have we all survived these circumstances by the total grace of God, but the Lord has used them all for His glory, and has given us a testimony for His Name's sake. Now I understand that no matter what happens in life, and tragedies do happen to believers and unbelievers alike, still the goodness and mercy of the Lord is very present, following us as we walk through whatever we have to walk through, making sense of the senseless and giving deep meaning and lasting truth to unexplainable circumstances.

I was born in New Jersey, in the United States, into a Jewish family. My grandparents came from Eastern Europe and my father and mother were both born in America. They held very strongly to Jewish tradition and when I was growing up we went regularly to the synagogue and we celebrated the Jewish holidays. We therefore always had a very strong identity. We knew that we were Jews before we were anything else; before we were Americans, we were Jews. Our extended family numbered between seventy and a hundred (because my father was one of six children and there were many cousins). When we gathered together for the holidays, at a typical Passover Seder[10] there would be at least seventy people there. It was fantastic!

I went to a public school[11] where the whole neighbourhood and all the surrounding neighbourhoods were Jewish. Three times a week, after public school, I went to Hebrew school. There we received Jewish instruction, we learned the beginnings of the Hebrew language, and we learned how to read from the Jewish prayer book which is called the Siddur. I did that until I was thirteen years old.

My parents expected me to marry a nice Jewish businessman and be a mother and a wife and live in the suburbs! They expected me to go to college, but that wasn't as important as being married to a nice Jewish businessman!

For some reason I always knew that life wasn't going to work out for me in that way. I was a non-conformist, and so were my brother and sister (I was the youngest of three children).

We were spiritual seekers. From the age of eleven I was looking for God. I remember sitting in my room when I felt a breeze coming through the window. I said to God, "If you are real then I want to know you." When I went to Hebrew school I heard Bible stories and I learned about a God who spoke to Moses and Abraham and told them what their purpose was. I wanted to know what my purpose was: why had I been born into this world? What did God want me to do?

From a young age, a Jewish person instinctively knows a couple of things: firstly, that Jesus is not for Jews – that is not a possibility. Rather, Jesus is for the Gentiles, for the Christians. Secondly, Jews are supposed to remain Jewish for their entire life. You are expected to live as a Jew and to die as a Jew.

During the 1960s and 1970s, when I was a teenager, the New Age movement[12] arrived, and that was permissible for Jewish people. In fact, it attracted many Jewish people. My sister and I were very close, even though she was eight years older than me, and together we began to seek spiritually in many of these groups. We were quite willing to experiment with whatever was put in front of us and so we went from one New Age philosophy, practice, and group to the next. Drugs were also involved. We were always rebellious and could never conform. As far as we were concerned, we were seeking God with all of our hearts.

I studied at New York University. My sister was also living in New York City and so we saw a great deal of each other and pursued our spiritual search together. We studied with the Jehovah's Witnesses for a time before moving on to study with the Mormons. My sister even became a Catholic and began going to a Catholic church. But when she took me to the Catholic church I felt it was just religion, like Judaism, and I knew it wasn't what I was looking for.

At that time, a revival sprang up. Today they call it the Jesus People revival.[13] It was amazing because you really did feel the presence of God on the streets of New York City. Wherever I went people were witnessing about Jesus, and as a result folk were getting saved. Hippies were getting saved. Even gang members were getting saved! This movement began to affect the lives of thousands of young people.

One day my sister, the person I trusted and felt closest to, came to talk to me. She told me she had received Jesus as her Saviour and I had to receive Him also because I was a sinner! It felt as though she was stuffing the Bible down my throat, and for the first time in our lives I had to disagree with her. "I cannot receive Him," I said, "I'm Jewish!" which was ironic, because I was open to every other cult and practice. I would pray to every Hindu god, but I could not receive Jesus. And so, for the first time in our lives, my sister and I parted company.

It was then that the Lord began to reveal Himself to me. I felt my sin was a heavy burden on my shoulders and I could feel myself sliding into a deep depression. Having been heavily involved in the occult I started to see demonic beings in my apartment, which frightened me. There were days I could not get up to go to work.

It was Easter time and some programmes appeared on the television about Jesus. As I started watching I was drawn to the person of Jesus and, strangely enough, I began to love Him. My sister and some of her Jewish friends who had become believers were going to a Messianic congregation on the lower east side of Manhattan that David was also going to. They invited me to go with them, but I still refused to talk to my sister and wouldn't go there. But it all became too much for me and one day I went into my apartment and said, "Lord Jesus, if you are the Messiah then I need you," and at that moment something came into my heart. Today I know that was the Holy Spirit.

My heart overflowed with love, joy, and peace and I felt the heavy burden of my sin being lifted off my shoulders. In front of my eyes I saw a blackboard with my life on it and it was being erased. I knew in that moment I had been "born again",[14] even though I had never read those words in the Bible, and then I saw a "veil" being taken away from my eyes.[15] And I had never read that in the Bible either!

In that instant I became a believer, and whereas before I had never wanted to go to that Messianic congregation with my sister, now I counted the minutes and seconds until the next meeting! I began to read the Bible voraciously. I took all of my New Age books and threw them away; I destroyed them because I didn't want anybody else to use them. I began going to the Messianic fellowship and they became my family.

I realized that one day I would have to confront my parents with this news, and I knew it would be very difficult.

One of the first things that happened to me after my experience of being "born again" was that I met my husband! I was part of this small congregation, run by an elderly Jewish pastor and his wife, that included Puerto Ricans, Chinese, a guy who had been in the Black Panther organization, and other Jewish people like myself. David Ortiz was one of the first people I met there. A couple of months later we fell in love and immediately knew we were going to get married, so we got engaged! All this happened without my parents' knowledge.

The day came when I had to go and see them and tell them that I was a believer in Jesus.

They didn't understand. And when I introduced them to David and told them I was going to get married they were still firmly convinced that I should marry a Jewish person. My father told me that if I went ahead with this "crazy religion" as well as marrying David, then I would be disowned. I knew he was telling me the truth because my father was a person who if he said it, he did it, and he would never go back on his word. I told him that while I was sorry he couldn't accept my decisions, even so, I believed it was God's will for my life. He didn't understand that at all and told me he would never talk to me again. And that was it. We left the house not knowing when we would see my parents again.

It was a difficult time. I became ill with pneumonia; it was like an emotional response to what had happened. But then the Lord began to minister to me from the Bible and I understood the words of Jesus when He said:

> "I tell you the truth … no-one who has left home or brothers or sisters or mother or father or children or fields for me and the gospel will fail to receive a hundred times as much in this present age (homes, brothers, sisters, mothers, children and fields – and with them, persecutions) and in the age to come, eternal life."[16]

When His mother and brothers came to visit Yeshua and wanted to see Him, He said:

"Who is my mother, and who are my brothers?"
Pointing to his disciples, he said, "Here are my
mother and my brothers. For whoever does the will
of my Father in heaven is my brother and sister and
mother."[17]

And so, in a very real sense, the Body of Messiah became my family. My sister who was also a believer was disowned by our father too. David and I married. My father refused to speak to me for years, but when the grandchildren came, my mother wanted to see me. We met occasionally and she would spend some time with her grandchildren. But then the day came when I had to tell her that we were going to move to Israel.

David was called to Israel first. One of the first things he said to me when we were dating was, "You know, I have a calling to go and live in Israel, and if you marry me you have to be prepared to come too!"

I had been to Israel when I was a teenager, before I was a believer. It was very interesting. As I toured the land with a group from my college, something came into my heart for the land; it was a connection to the land itself that I had never felt when I had been living in the United States. However, I detested the Israelis! They seemed to me to be so different culturally to American Jews and I had some really bad experiences with them. I came back saying, "I love the land but I will never live there!" So when David talked about going to live in Israel, I thought, well, we'll get married, we'll get settled, we'll get established, we'll have children, and he'll forget all about it.

We got married and we had children, but we were never able to get settled and we were never able to get established in the United States. David kept talking about how everything that was taking place with us was preparation for Israel, including his studies in dental technology.

"I'm not going to live in Israel," I told him, "but if you want the Lord to speak to me about living in Israel then you're going to have to be quiet and never talk about it again so that the Lord can speak to me."

Anybody who knows David Ortiz knows he can never be quiet about anything! But he never said another word after that! And the Lord began to deal with me in so many ways. We also began to meet Israelis, and by the time we left the US and made aliyah[18] to Israel in 1985, I was not just 100 per cent sure, I was 1,000 per cent sure that this was God's will for our lives. We shared a burning desire to preach the gospel to the Jewish people. They were my people and David had been raised with Orthodox Jews. He knew much more about Orthodox Judaism than I did when I met him. He had been immersed into that culture and society from childhood. So that was our calling, to share the gospel with the Jewish people.

Looking back, I have no regrets. There are many things that have happened to us throughout the years but I have never regretted moving to Israel because I have always known that the best and safest place for a marriage and family and any kind of work you do for the Lord is to be in the centre of God's will. So long as I knew we were in the centre of God's will there couldn't be any regrets, because whatever has happened, I have always stood on the verse:

> And we know that in all things God works for the good of those who love him, who have been called according to his purpose.[19]

Fourteen years passed and my father still would not speak to me. I realized that many people had given me words of encouragement from the Lord that one day we would be reconciled. After eleven or twelve years this still wasn't happening and I was asking the Lord, why? I came to realize He had to do something in my own life before He could re-establish my relationship with my father, and that involved having a deeper relationship with Him as my heavenly Father before my earthly father could come back into the picture.

Then my mother made contact to say she wanted to see us and she offered to pay for all of us to visit America. We had five children at that time. My parents were living in Florida but she was going to meet us in New York. However, a few days before we were due to arrive she injured her back and my father wouldn't let her travel. Instead, he offered to arrange for us to stay in a hotel near to where they lived, although he remained adamant that he would not meet us.

So we arrived in Florida. My mother was going back and forth between us and my father. One day she said to us, "I'm not going to tell you what to do, but he sits at the pool every day between eight and nine o'clock in the morning. David encouraged me to go and see him. Taking the children with me, I walked down the beach to his apartment house and there he was, sitting by the pool. We hadn't seen each other for fourteen years and he had never seen my children.

I said, "Hi Dad, I've missed you."

"Well, that's been your fault," he replied.

"I just wanted to say hi and introduce you to my kids."

He stood up and one by one took each child's face in his hands and looked into their eyes.

"I would like to hug you," I said to him. So we hugged and we left and we came back to Israel.

A month later, in August 1990, Saddam Hussein invaded Kuwait, initiating the Gulf War. Every week my parents would call me and say, "There's going to be a war; your children are going to die. Come back to Florida and we'll buy you a house!"

So finally, one day as I put down the phone, I felt I should take the children to Florida for the duration of the war while David stayed in Israel. We flew to Florida and moved into an apartment. One day my father walked in, and it was as though all the previous years had been erased. After the war, when David came to join us, before we all few back to Israel together, we talked to my parents about Yeshua and continued to visit them every summer until 2006. My sister was also reconciled to our parents.

It was when my father was dying that he called for my sister and me to visit him; he wanted to talk about Yeshua. He was afraid to die because he knew he was about to enter eternity unprepared. The night before he died he saw the Lord. A night nurse was with him who also happened to be a believer. He said to her, "I see a man."

"Who is it?" she asked him.

"It's the Lord," he replied. She led him through the Sinner's Prayer[20] and at the end he said, "in Jesus' name, Amen." A few hours later he went into a coma, and twelve hours later he died and went to eternity with the Lord. It was a miracle.

Since living in Israel, we have been very mission minded as well as running a congregation here in Ariel. In addition, the Lord opened a way for us to witness to Palestinians. That was a little bit difficult for me in the beginning and the Lord had to do a work of forgiveness in my heart because I realized that all my life I had learned with every fibre of my being that the Arab people were my enemies. I realized that I did not care for their souls and I did not love them, but I knew I was wrong to continue that way because the Holy Spirit was moving among the villages and many were getting saved. But in a moment of time, the Lord gave me His love for them, and my enemies became my brothers and sisters. Through the love of God we have had incredible fellowship and have experienced the "one new man",[21] the gospel to the Muslims, and the gospel to the Jews. It's been an amazing experience.

CHAPTER 2

David and Leah Ortiz in Israel

I will bring you from the nations and gather you from the countries where you have been scattered.[22]

For more than a hundred years Jewish people have been immigrating in their thousands to Israel from nations around the world where they have been living since the Romans dispersed the Jews from Israel in AD 70. It would seem perverse not to acknowledge the many biblical prophecies, made centuries earlier, that refer to this unique occurrence that is ongoing today. In seeking answers to the question, what is God doing in Israel today, the return of the Jewish diaspora to Israel in recent times has to be one of the answers.

But what does life hold for them when they return? It would appear that with every person who arrives to live in Israel from another nation there is a story; a story of being drawn, as if by a magnet, to a land they can call their homeland.

However, David and Leah Ortiz's story illustrates the struggle that is involved in making the transition from a country like America to live in Israel where Judaism is the state religion and where life can be extremely difficult for Jewish believers in Yeshua, Jesus. And it is easy to see why. For centuries, Judaism has fulfilled a function. It has provided the Jewish diaspora with their own unique identity and sense of community while living as aliens in foreign lands. Wherever there has been a Jewish community in the world, there has been a synagogue. Celebrating Jewish traditions and the biblical feasts gave Jews their own collective memory of being a people who once had a land of their own. "Next year in Jerusalem," they would pray at the end of every Passover Seder; Jerusalem was the focus of their longing. Psalm 137, the well-known lament of the Babylonian Jews, describes their deep sense of loss and longing to be back in the land:

> **By the rivers of Babylon we sat and wept**
> **when we remembered Zion …**
> **If I forget you, Jerusalem,**
> **may my right hand forget its skill.**
> **May my tongue cling to the roof of my mouth**
> **if I do not remember you,**
> **if I do not consider Jerusalem**
> **my highest joy.**

So when David and Leah decided to move from the relative comfort of the United States of America to be "missionaries" in Israel to both Jewish and Arab/Palestinian people, they knew they would be entering a land where

Messianic believers were very much in the minority and where Judaism was an overwhelmingly strong influence and quite opposed to belief in Yeshua, Jesus. What was it that compelled them to make what would prove to be a difficult and costly move?

David's story continued …

I told Leah from the beginning that we could only get married if she agreed to come to Israel with me! I explained to her that I believed two people could not walk together unless they shared the same vision. She agreed. Then later on she disagreed! And then she agreed again and eventually we started to make plans to move to Israel with our three young children.

Leaving America involved some major heart searching on my part. I remember being in a prayer meeting where I felt the Lord was showing me that I was not ready to leave. This surprised me as I had always thought Leah was the one delaying our departure! As I considered this, and prayed some more, I felt the Lord was telling me, "It's you: you're not ready. Emotionally you're not ready. You haven't forgiven completely yet. You still have an identity crisis. You don't have complete confidence in who you are and in my love for you. If you go to Israel, somebody is going to say 'boo' and you're going to run away; you're not secure enough yet."

So as I allowed God to work in my heart, His identity became my identity, and as issues came to the surface that I had to confront, with His help I was able to forgive and move forward, confident that God loved me and would take care of us.

We arrived in Israel with our three children and moved to Beer Sheva. Within the next eight years we had three more children. When we first arrived I worked in my profession as a dental technician. It became clear there were more opportunities in my area of expertise further north so we decided to move. By this time there were communities of believers living in Jerusalem and Tiberias but we felt it right to move to a place where we could start a new congregation.

As we were travelling around Israel looking for somewhere to live, one day we arrived in Ariel and we immediately felt that it was the right place for us. We found an apartment and made contact with four Messianic Jewish families who were living here at that time. They welcomed us but at the same time warned us, "Don't tell anybody that you believe in Jesus – we don't want any trouble. Our children go to school. We've bought beautiful homes here and we don't want any problems with this society because they like us and we've made some good friends."

I replied, "Jesus didn't say be careful when people persecute you. Rather He said, be careful when people speak well of you."[23] I told them I could not agree with their position as I didn't want to be ashamed of the name of Jesus.

So we told our neighbours that we believed in Yeshua.

About three months later the local rabbi came to see us along with his associates, all dressed in black.

We spent an hour together and he warned us that he would not allow us to talk about Yeshua in Ariel. I replied that the last time I looked, Israel was a democracy and not the Soviet Union and that I would exercise my democratic rights to talk freely about what I believe.

"If you do," he said, "I will make so much trouble for you that you won't know what to do with yourself."

I said, "That's OK, I will talk about Yeshua."

At that time I had my own dental laboratory. The rabbi instructed all the dentists in Ariel not to give me work. From then on the dentists told me, "We do not give work to missionaries," and I received no further orders for my services from them. The religious Jews attempted to have our children taken out of the school they were enrolled in by telling the principal (head teacher) that they were children of missionaries and should be thrown out of school. However, the principal told them that the school was not a religious establishment and that as long as our children were in the school, they were under her protection. She later told us about this conversation and warned us to be careful.

These same religious Jews organized a protest in the street in front of our apartment. They used loudspeakers to warn our neighbours, "These are missionaries. Get them out of here."

The mayor at the time responded to this intimidation by saying, "This is not a banana state. Rather we are a state that obeys the law. If you want to get rid of these people then hire a lawyer and do this through the courts." So they drew up a petition, and the lawyers advised them that if enough people signed it, by law we would have to sell our apartment and leave Ariel.

Seeing and hearing the mob in the street below our apartment was very frightening for our children because they had to go to school the next day. So I told them what we would do: we were going to remember and believe the verse, "I am not ashamed of the gospel, because it is the power [dynamite] of God for the salvation of everyone who believes: first for the Jew, then for the Gentile."[24]

"Tomorrow," I told them, "when you go to school, this means you are not going to walk with your face to the ground. Rather you are going to walk with your head up high. You are going to look those people in the eye because we are not ashamed of the man on the cross. If we respect what we believe, people will respect us too because Jesus said, 'He who receives you receives me, and he who receives me receives the one who sent me.' "[25] I told them that when Jesus walked into a crowd He didn't take a poll to see who liked Him and who did not. Rather He kept on looking at His Father for approval. "If we do the same," I encouraged them, "we are going to be fine."

We experienced a lot of trouble in the town and many malicious and untrue rumours were spread about us.

One day a man came to our door and said, "You and I are going to go downstairs and fight. My wife became a believer because of you. And now that she

38

has betrayed Judaism you and I are going to fight."
He started cursing.

So I said to him, "Listen, there are children in the
house. Please don't curse in this way."

He said, "Come downstairs and fight."

I thought about what I should do because I don't
come from a tradition of not hitting back! As I walked
down the stairs I decided it was best just to let him hit
me – I would not hit him back because if I did, it would
just be because of my pride. I thought of the verse in
Philippians that describes how Jesus left His glory and
became a man of no reputation.[26]

Stepping out into the street, I looked for him,
but he was not there! He had gone! However, for
the next two years every time he saw me he would
start to curse and shout, "Get away from my wife." I
never responded to him and many people wondered
why I didn't defend myself in the face of such strong
accusations. They would tell me to say something to
silence him. But I always kept my mouth shut.

Two years later he came to our home again and
said to Leah, "Where's David? I want to talk to him."

I wondered why he had come and anticipated more
trouble, but when I went downstairs to see him he
said, "I have come to apologize to you. I have cursed
you and embarrassed you and tried to do whatever I
could to destroy you. I am sorry. The name of Buddha
doesn't bother me. Muhammad doesn't bother me.
But the name of Yeshua, Jesus, irritates me, and after
my wife became a believer and talked about Jesus,
I blamed you. But now I have come to tell you that I

am sorry." He gave me a kiss on the cheek – he's from Morocco! – and invited our family to visit his home that night for dinner.

When we had finished our meal and were about to leave, he told us we couldn't possibly go home because it was too late. Rather we had to stay the night in his house. He proceeded to lay rugs on the floor and said we would have breakfast together the next morning. Today he is reading the New Testament and we are very good friends!

Leah's story continued …

There are some things in life you cannot prepare for, and for David and me, it was the day our son Ami was critically injured by a bomb.

A Danish group had been volunteering in the hotel in Ariel doing some repairs and redecoration, and before going home they asked if we would take them on a sightseeing tour of Jerusalem. I arranged a tour for 20 March 2008, and at the time I made the plans, I didn't realize that that day coincided with the Feast of Purim.[27] Normally I never go on such trips because I have multiple sclerosis and it is very hard for me to walk up and down the hills of Jerusalem. However, on that particular morning David and I got up and we left the apartment together. Ami was planning to go to school as usual that day, but after we left, he turned over and went back to sleep! He was the only one of our children living at home at that time.

At two o'clock in the afternoon, Ami called me to say he hadn't gone to school because he had overslept. I was really upset with him. Then he told me that somebody had left a Purim package (it's called Mishloach Manot in Hebrew) full of candies that looked beautiful and could he open it. He added that he didn't know who had left it by the door to our apartment, but I agreed that he could bring it in and open it to see who it was from, all the while chiding him that he hadn't gone to school. And with that we hung up.

Fifteen minutes later, another of our sons, who was at that time in the army, called me to say that a terror attack had occurred in Ariel. A few minutes later he called back to say it had happened on our street. When I called Ami, there was no answer. I then called a young lady who had been cleaning our apartment earlier that day and a policeman answered. He told me that there had been an explosion in our home and that our son was being rushed to hospital and we had to get there as quickly as we could.

I screamed at him, "Is he alive?"

He said, "Just get to the hospital immediately."

Leaving our Danish group, we jumped into a taxi and arrived at the hospital forty minutes later. Our family had gathered there and when we walked in we met the doctors who took us aside and told us that Ami's life was in danger. He was about to undergo an operation but we were warned he might not survive.

The police were also there and they informed David that a bomb had been placed in the Purim basket that

Ami had unwrapped on our kitchen table. The bomb had detonated and Ami had taken the full force of the explosion. They were keen to know whether David had any idea who might have left this bomb so they could start their investigation.

Meanwhile, Ami was wheeled into the operating theatre and the surgeons fought for eight hours to save his life. That was the first of fourteen operations he was to undergo in the next three years.

As we were sitting in the waiting room, numb from shock, people who had heard the news were arriving from Ariel. Believers came. Our family was there. I asked if anybody had a Bible. Somebody gave me a small book of Psalms. I turned to Psalm 36 and it was a Rhema word from God to me: as I read the words it was as though God was speaking directly to me. It talks about the sinfulness of the wicked; people who do crimes because they hate:

> There is no fear of God
> before his eyes.
> For in his own eyes he flatters himself
> too much to detect or hate his sin.
> The words of his mouth are wicked and deceitful;
> he has ceased to be wise and to do good.
> Even on his bed he plots evil;
> he commits himself to a sinful course
> and does not reject what is wrong ...
> May the foot of the proud not come against me,
> nor the hand of the wicked drive me away.
> See how the evildoers lie fallen –
> thrown down, not able to rise![28]

And the Lord spoke to my heart that this was a hate crime. The final verses were very significant for me:

> May the foot of the proud not come against me,
> nor the hand of the wicked drive me away.

And the Lord spoke to my heart, "You are not to move from Ariel," because the first thing I wanted to do was to run away as far as I could from Ariel. It also said:

> See how the evildoers lie fallen –
> thrown down, not able to rise!

And again the Lord spoke to my heart, "The one who did this is destroyed, but I want him to be saved." And that same love of God that He had given me for the Palestinians, my enemies, I felt all of a sudden above my head again and I realized the Lord wanted to give me His love for the person who had done this to my son. It took me a few minutes, but I remembered what had happened with the Palestinians, how the Lord had used it for His glory. I allowed Him to give me His love and forgiveness for that person, whoever he was, and the Lord impressed on my heart that I was to pray for his salvation every day, which we have tried to do ever since.

Every single person in our family has had to come to that place of forgiveness, including Ami.

But that evening something else very significant happened. Finally, at two o'clock in the morning, we were able to go and see Ami. He was in the Intensive Care Unit of a children's hospital called Schneider Children's Medical Centre, in Petach Tikvah, and when we saw him it was a dreadful sight to see. His face was swollen; he was covered in bandages. He had been wounded from the top of his head to the bottom of his feet. He had second- and third-degree burns all over his body. He had more than one hundred pieces of glass and shrapnel in his body and in his eyes. He had a hole in his chest that was so big you could see his lungs breathing. Three toes had been blown off, and skin and muscle from his stomach and thighs had also been blown off. He was hooked up to many tubes, and the doctors told us we would talk further in the morning about his injuries, but now they advised us to get some rest.

As it was a children's hospital we were able to be there all the time as there were beds for parents. But it was when we went to lie down that night that we really went into crisis. I felt my mind splinter into a thousand directions at the same time, and I didn't have the power to gather my thoughts and bring them back. I told David, "I'm losing it."

David said he felt like he'd fallen into a pit that was so deep he would never get out of it. How could he get out of that pit after what had happened?

Then all of a sudden, as he prayed and cried out to God, David saw the Lord. And as he saw what he saw, and heard what he heard, he whispered to me in my ear what he was experiencing. He said that he saw the Lord sitting on His throne and he knew that everything was under His control. And then he said he saw the angel of death trying to enter our home and the Lord said, "You cannot have him." And although his life was in grave danger, we knew Ami would live.

The Lord spoke to David and said, "A decision has been made in heaven that you will not understand, but I have decided to glorify Myself and Ami is going to be fine. Ami is going to be fine. Ami is going to be fine. He's going to walk out of this hospital."

It was so real. God's presence was so evident that we were able to get up and wash our faces and eat something. A few hours later we would sit down with the doctor.

In the morning when we met with the doctor he started by telling us that Ami had experienced a miracle. "Last night," he said, "we didn't know what was going to happen: his life was in danger. But this morning all of his systems have stabilized. He is still extremely critical but he is stable." Then he proceeded to tell us about Ami's injuries and warned us that it was going to be a long and difficult recovery.

However, Ami remained stable from that moment on.

News about what had happened spread quickly throughout Israel and the world through the internet. People worldwide were praying for Ami. Israelis – believers and non-believers – started to arrive in the waiting room outside the Intensive Care Unit. On average we had eighty people a day bringing us food, drinks, and flowers. Groups of believers were praying for Ami morning, noon, and night in the waiting room. Many people who lived in Ariel came to visit us and every one of them came to us and said, "We don't know why we're saying this but we know that Ami is going to be OK."

We knew it was because the Lord had said, "Ami is going to be fine." Believers and unbelievers felt it. Every one of our family had to come to that place of forgiveness, and when I asked our children why they were able to forgive, they replied because they knew Ami was going to be fine. We knew we had to forgive in order to heal from the trauma of this experience. We understood that if we did not forgive, we would be victims twice.

After eight days Ami woke from his induced coma. The doctors had warned us that they didn't know how his mind would react to the damage his body had suffered. When he opened his eyes, the first thing he said to me was, "Did the Orthodox Jews do this to me?" From the start the police had asked us whether we had any idea who would have planted this bomb outside our door. At first we thought it might have been put there by some Palestinians who had a grudge against us for preaching the gospel in Muslim areas. But the police were convinced the perpetrator was Jewish.

We told Ami that yes, it would seem that an Orthodox Jew had done this to him, but we also told him that we had to forgive. Later he told us that forgiveness was just given to him and so he was able to forgive. I was with him every day during his recovery and can confirm that he showed no bitterness; he didn't even have nightmares or flashbacks. The Lord delivered him from so much and he began to heal rapidly. The doctors were amazed at his rate of recovery. We knew it was because people were praying for him all over the world. And as we began to send out updates to people, every operation that he went through was a success. He had fourteen reconstructive surgeries to his body. He had skin grafts. His eardrums had been blown out and had to be replaced. He had extensive nerve damage in his arms, especially his left arm which caused severe pain in his hand. As far as playing basketball was concerned (he had been a basketball player since the age of eight – he is very tall, six foot six or 1.98 m), the doctors warned us that he would not be able to play high-level competitive basketball again.

After five and a half months Ami walked out of that hospital and came home. His basketball coach called and asked him to come back to the training sessions. When Ami told him he couldn't even open his hands to hold a basketball, the coach replied that when he had been serving in the Israeli army in Lebanon, a grenade had blown up next to him and he had suffered many of the same injuries that Ami had. He said, "I know what you have to do – just come back to basketball."

The first time Ami caught the ball he was in tremendous pain, and when he tried to run he fell flat on his face. I was talking to the coach one day and said, "It's too hard for him." But he replied that in every practice Ami could do something he hadn't been able to do the practice before and that in three months he would be back on the court. Well, in one month he was back on the court playing, running, and jumping and doing everything the doctors said he wouldn't be able to do!

At the same time the Lord used this experience for us to be able to talk about Yeshua here in Israel. Ami's story was featured in the newspapers. David and I were interviewed on television and on radio.

Eighteen months after the incident, the person who had done this was caught. His name is Jack Teitel, and he is an Orthodox Jew from the United States who had made aliyah in the year 2000. He had also murdered two Palestinian Arabs in cold blood and had laid explosive packages in different places in Israel against people he considered to be false prophets or people who were endangering Jewish people with their philosophies, or their religion, or whatever he decided was wrong. He claimed that God had told him to do these things.

The legal process lasted three years. We went to every hearing that we could. Ami came with us to one hearing. Jack Teitel's lawyers tried to prove that he was insane. But the judges would not accept this and in the end he was sentenced to more than ninety years in prison. One day, if the Lord makes it possible, we would be open and willing to go and visit him to share the gospel with him.

CHAPTER 3

Muslim-background Believers Living in the West Bank and Israel

Despite being branded as "missionaries", David and Leah Ortiz continued to share their faith in Yeshua with the Jewish community in their home town of Ariel. At the same time they started to turn their attention to the Muslim Palestinians living in the villages surrounding Ariel. To his amazement, David was able to make contact with many Muslim people who were willing to hear about Jesus, although entering these Islamic villages to give away Bibles proved to be a dangerous activity. For a Muslim person living in the West Bank to renounce Islam and embrace the God of Israel is a brave and costly step, as this chapter reveals; yet it is happening. Could this be another indication of what God is doing in Israel and the wider Middle East in these days?

As news about these Muslim-background believers (MBBs) started to emerge, I was looking for an opportunity to meet some of these people. I was meeting Israeli Arab

Christians in Jerusalem who were visiting Palestinian towns and villages in the West Bank that were entirely Islamic, and they were telling me about reports they were hearing of considerable numbers of Muslim people having dreams about Jesus. They also told me about Muslims who were becoming believers in Jesus through Christian programmes they were seeing or hearing on the internet. I can recall a number of conversations with these Israeli Arab Christians who were concerned for the growing number of Muslims who were showing an interest in knowing more about Jesus but had no means of meeting Christians with whom they could study the Bible; indeed, they did not have access to a Bible.

It is a sad state of affairs that many Christians, particularly those living in the West, take sides – they are either pro-Israel or pro-Palestinian. As a result, those who are pro-Israel and hold a strong Christian Zionist position (as opposed to a biblical Zionist attitude) at best ignore the Israeli Arab and Palestinian community and at worst believe that all Palestinians are Islamic terrorists bent on destroying Israel and the Jewish people. In the same way, those Christians who are pro-Palestinian have hostile feelings towards Israel (and as Israel is a Jewish state one can conclude that to hold such a view is to be anti-Jewish).

I was keen to discover the truth about Muslims becoming believers in Jesus in the West Bank areas where the Palestinian Authority has control. If God is supernaturally revealing Himself to Muslim people living in the West Bank, it begs the question, why? Could it be that these people who were once hostile towards Israel and Jewish people to the point of wanting to kill every Jew are now having a change of heart? Indeed, one is left wondering how the political and religious climate could change if vast numbers of Muslims were to start to believe in Jesus and embrace the God of Israel.

This aim of this book is to investigate what God is doing in Israel today. The opportunity to meet two MBBs presented itself recently when I visited David and Leah Ortiz in Ariel and David offered to arrange a rendezvous with two men, former Muslims, later that afternoon.

It takes a strong feeling of conviction to be prepared to risk danger, even your life, to share your faith with people who will most probably hate you. I was interested to find out what prompted David Ortiz to get into his car and drive out of Ariel towards a nearby Palestinian village, not knowing who he would meet or what would happen.

David Ortiz takes up the story ...

It was because the Israelis gave me so much trouble here in Ariel that I decided to go to the Gentiles. I have an Israeli Jewish friend called Doron, who is also a Messianic believer, and we decided to visit some of the Palestinian villages around Ariel. At that time I had a car that worked by faith! It was a 1976 Volkswagen. My neighbour said to me one day, "You know, David, your car reminds me of Moses: each time you turn on the engine, white smoke comes out – the cloud is following you wherever you go!"

One morning, Doron and I drove to a local Arab village and we started giving away Bibles in Arabic.

A curious crowd soon gathered around us. However, when they realized that the books we were giving away were Bibles, they became hostile and started to hit us. "Jihad, Jihad," they shouted as their hostility turned to rage. They wanted to kill us.

Somehow we managed to get back inside the car, but they tried to pull us out through the windows. An older man stuck his head through the window and yelled at us, "Today you're going to die."

I believed him. So I said, "Lord, here I am. I'm ready. Into your hands I commit my spirit, my time has come."

Doron said, "David, start the car."

I said, "Doron, the car won't start unless we are pushed."

"David, you have to try."

So I turned the key but the engine just whirred. When the crowd realized the car wouldn't start they really got into a frenzy and started throwing stones to shatter the windows in order to pull us out. But the windows didn't break!

Doron said, "Keep trying to start the engine."

By God's grace the car did start and we slowly started to move. But there were so many men on the car and hanging on to it that we couldn't see where we were going. Eventually, as we gathered speed, they released their hold and we were able to drive away.

Once outside the village and out of the Palestinian Authority controlled area, I stopped the car. We climbed out, knelt down, kissed the ground, and gave thanks to God for getting us out of that village alive.

The next day when I saw Doron, he said, "David, we did not leave that village in a good way. Let's go back and talk to them."

"You're right," I agreed, "Let's go back."

So we pushed the car to get it started, jumped back in and drove to the centre of the village. When we arrived, the place was empty apart from four Palestinian men sitting around a table, talking together.

I switched off the engine and we got out of the car. When the men saw us, they looked surprised and it was clear they recognized us. Slowly they got up from their chairs and started walking towards us.

"Why have you come back?" one of them said.

"We forgot to tell you something," I replied.

He said, "Is it that important?"

"It's very important."

"Well, if it's that important, come to my house and we'll drink tea and talk about it."

Doron and I followed him and entered his home, and there we talked to him about Jesus. "This is amazing," he said. "I want you to talk to my brother."

So we went to the brother's house. This brother said, "This is amazing. I want you to talk to my other brother."

This continued until we had spoken to all eight brothers and various cousins, and as we continued to return to this village and many other villages in the area, and to witness, many of these men accepted the Lord.

> In our experience, the Palestinians come to the Lord very quickly, and we know more than 150 who have become believers since that first visit. Life is not easy for them. In fact, some of them lost their lives when they renounced Islam and became believers in Jesus.

Throughout our lunch together, David had been constantly on his mobile phone to the two men we were hoping to meet later that afternoon. Owing to the security zones within the West Bank, arranging these meetings was complicated, even risky. There are three security zones in the West Bank: A, B, and C. Zone A, which represents 3 per cent of the West Bank, is under full civil and security control by the Palestinian Authority. This area includes eight Palestinian cities and their surrounding areas (Nablus, Jenin, Tulkarem, Qalqilya, Ramallah, Bethlehem, Jericho, and 80 per cent of Hebron). No Jewish people live in these areas, and entry into these areas is forbidden to all Israeli citizens.

Zone B, which covers approximately 25 per cent of the West Bank, is under the civil control of the Palestinian Authority and joint Israeli–Palestinian security control. Included in this zone are more than 400 Palestinian villages, but no Jewish people live here.

Zone C, which includes the remaining 72 per cent of the West Bank, is under full Israeli civil and security control and is home to several towns and villages where Jewish people live. Ariel is in Zone C and surrounded by Palestinian towns and villages that are entirely Islamic, and increasingly fundamentalist in their attitude to people of other faiths, whether Jewish or Christian.

And so we set off and proceeded to drive west, out of Ariel into another "zone".

David explained that the first man we were to meet was walking five kilometres from his home village to meet us in an area of "no man's land". He was having to be careful to make sure he wasn't being followed, and we would not be able to park in a lay-by and wait for him to appear as that would attract unwanted attention from the Palestinian Authority or Israeli security who may enquire who we were and why we had stopped. As we drove out of Ariel, road signs told us we were leaving Zone C. We passed other signs, to villages in Zone B or C; a wrong turn could have been dangerous for us.

Eventually the call came through and David knew where our first man was waiting in hiding for us. Driving slowly along a particular stretch of road, he stopped by a row of bushes. A man appeared and jumped into the back of the car. David sped away before anybody else who happened to be driving along would see us, and after a short distance took a turn to the left onto a rough track. We stopped behind some trees, out of view of passing traffic.

If all this sounds tense, it was! I have visited Israel, including the West Bank and Gaza, scores of times, and some of those visits have been during times of trouble and war. But this was the first time I had felt a tangible sense of fear, and it was because the man sitting in the back seat of the car was risking his life to come and meet us.

So who was he? David spoke to him in Hebrew as it is their common language. In order to protect his identity we shall refer to him as "M". This is what he told us.

First of all I want to thank God for giving me the way of life through Him. My aim is to have a Bible in every Palestinian home so we, the Palestinian people, can have the true peace, because when we start believing in Yeshua, that's when we have real peace.

I came to faith in 1995. During that time David Ortiz came to my village and was giving away Bibles in the street. At that time I didn't even know what the Bible was. I saw a mob around him and watched these men eagerly taking the books from him. I said to him, "What is that book?" The books were disappearing fast, so I asked if I could have several copies; I wanted to be able to give one to each of my brothers.

He gave me several books and a card with his mobile phone number and told me that if I had any questions, to call him and we would sit down and talk together.

I went to my house with the books. One of my brothers was there and I told him how I had seen a man in the village giving out these books. We sat down together and were curious to see what the books were about. I opened one of the books – it was the first time we had ever seen or read the Bible. We found ourselves reading verses from the gospel of Matthew chapter five where Jesus was talking about loving your enemies. We had never read such words before. Love your enemies? We were stunned. We stared into each other's eyes wondering what this message could mean.

My brother said, "What kind of message is this? It's

telling us to love our enemies; the people we want to kill and destroy, it says we should love."

All our lives we had been taught both at school and in the mosque that it is the duty of every Muslim to destroy and kill the Jews. So when we read this we wanted to know more about this message.

I told my brother that the person who had given me the books had also given me a card with his phone number. We both agreed that we needed to call him and arrange to meet so that we could sit down together and let him explain to us what this message means.

So I called David and told him that I needed to talk to him to learn more about the message in the book.

David came to my house with another Christian man, who spoke beautiful Arabic. We sat together with our whole family in the living room. The main question in our minds was how we could love people who we perceived wanted to destroy us. For two and a half hours we sat together asking questions and studying the Bible. Then we shared a meal; we had prepared dinner earlier. All the time they talked about the love of Yeshua. We had never heard such a message before.

From then on, every Thursday we went with David to Ramallah to meet and pray with other men who believed in Yeshua. They were from various countries and were working in the West Bank. We had walked into a different kind of world to what we were used to; we had walked into a world of love. These same believers started coming to our village and visiting us in our home, but it wasn't long before the Palestinian Authority started to notice that we had foreigners coming to our home. "Why do you have Christians coming to your house?" they asked us.

As soon as we were under suspicion and being watched, our situation became very unsafe. They [the PA] kidnapped my older brother; they took him and tortured him. He was in jail for two years. For the first seven months we didn't know whether he was dead or alive, they wouldn't tell us. It was a very difficult time for our family because we frequently saw the dead bodies of prisoners being dragged by cars through the streets. We knew that in the jails people were frequently executed without their family knowing. The only way they found out what had happened to their husbands, fathers, or sons was when their bodies were dumped in the streets in this way.

When my brother was arrested, all we could do was pray to God. We started sending messages to other believers we knew to pray for my brother's safety. Thank God, Jesus heard our prayers. One day in 2002 the Israeli army temporarily entered Nablus (Shechem) in an operation called Defensive Shield. Its aim was to destroy terrorist infrastructure after a series of devastating terror attacks and suicide bombings in Israel. During this operation, Israeli soldiers broke through the walls of the prison and freed some prisoners. God was gracious to our family; my brother was released. We later found out that his name had been on the list for execution but Jesus gave my brother a new life – a second chance to live.

However, it was not safe for my brother to return to his house so he stayed in Tel Aviv (where he had a permit to work). Today, by God's grace, he is in Norway with his family.

The PA then turned their attention to my other brother. They were determined to kill him; there was a fatwah[29] on him. He had to leave the family house and for two and a half years he slept in the fields and he slept in factories. It was very difficult for him. Eventually he also received religious asylum in Norway and today he is there with his family.

Persecution has made us stronger; it hasn't weakened us. My prayer and my focus is to have a copy of the Bible in every home in my village.

I asked "M" about his family and he told us that he was desperately praying for his children.

It is very dangerous for them in school where they are taught how to be a Jihadist. From a young age they are taught to hate Jews and that it is good to kill Jews and infidels. Our children are taught to kill and destroy. They are robbed of their childhood.

My wife has been excommunicated from her family because she believes in Yeshua. In Islam this is called betrayal and, according to Islamic law, deserves death. My prayer is that God will fill me with His power so that I can live for Him. I pray that many other Muslims will find Yeshua, but we have a very tense and dangerous atmosphere in my village at the present time. My brother evangelized in the village – that is why he was put in prison. At the moment, we have to be very careful.

There are Christians in the big towns like Ramallah and Bethlehem, but my village and the surrounding area is completely Islamic and fundamentalist.

Death in this situation is very close to me, but because I am so aware of God's presence, I do not feel afraid.

When my brother was in jail they [the PA] also arrested me. They told me that I had been seen walking around with a man called David Ortiz and they told me to stop seeing him. They told me that all the Christians who came to my house with David were CIA agents and I was forbidden to see these people again. "If you want to spare your life and not be like your brother, you are going to stop seeing them. We are going to be watching you all the time."

Things don't get easier, "M" told us; in fact, they get more difficult.

Before the PA started threatening me, the believing brothers used to come and visit me. Now I feel ashamed that I cannot invite you to my house, but it would be too dangerous. Look how we sit here in this car with David, afraid to be seen, hunted like animals.

Throughout these years I have refused to allow them [the PA] to coerce me or to be afraid, and by God's grace I am still alive.

Before we started the car to return "M" to the bushes where we had picked him up in no man's land, we prayed for his safety as he returned to his village. He had walked 5 km to meet with us and now had to retrace his steps. As we approached the bushes, David slowed the car and "M" jumped out and ran off.

David looked at his watch and reached for his mobile phone. It was time to rendezvous with our second appointment of the afternoon.

We found ourselves at a busy intersection where buses and lorries were pulling in and out of lay-bys, picking people up and dropping people off. To one side was an Israeli Army watchtower and checkpoint. To the other side, a petrol station. This was clearly a busy junction, but an ideal place where we could park for a while and blend into the activity that was going on all around us without attracting undue attention. One more phone call and it wasn't long before a man opened the back door of the car and climbed in. David greeted him and, again speaking in Hebrew rather than his native Arabic, he started to tell us his story. For the purposes of this book I am calling him "N".

I am so happy and so delighted that brothers and sisters come and visit me so that we can share fellowship. I believe these are my real brothers and sisters more than my biological family; brothers in Yeshua.

I live in a Muslim area. My father was an Islamic teacher. Even as a child I recognized that there was a vast emptiness in my life. I felt that emptiness all the time until one day a friend gave me a pamphlet. As I read it, a peace came over me and the emptiness I had been feeling started to disappear. It was like a cool and gentle breath which went from my head right through my body and brought such refreshment and hope to my mind.

I needed more books like this to read so my friend introduced me to David who, he told me, would give me more books. So I met David and we had a Bible study together. But it wasn't long before the intifada[30] started making it impossible to travel freely; at such times of heightened unrest between Palestinians and Israelis, the military frequently impose curfews that prevent us from leaving our homes and our villages. As a result, for a long time we were unable to meet. However, I used the Bible studies we had shared with people in my village.

Underneath my house I have a very big room. I put some chairs and tables in there and once a week I held a Bible study. We are not like Westerners; we Palestinians cannot meet or walk in groups any longer because it is seen as a sign of aggression and we are arrested. We have to be very careful not to draw attention to ourselves. However, I started giving out Bibles to individual people and we now have thirteen believers (MBBs) and we meet for a Bible study every week, but never on the same day. At first, when we met, the local people became curious and started looking in the windows to see what we were doing. When they realized we were studying the Bible, they began throwing stones at the house. My wife left the house because she felt it was too dangerous, and she went to stay with her family as she was afraid. I decided we had to do something differently and so now we never have the Bible study on the same day – each week we meet on a different day.

One night when I came back to my house, I opened the door and there was a letter. Inside was an empty cartridge of a bullet and a note which said, "We shot this bullet into the air, but if you keep on meeting David Ortiz, next time we will shoot this bullet into your heart. Keep away from David Ortiz."

I got into a panic. I didn't want to be a Muslim. I didn't want to be a Christian. I didn't want to live like this and I didn't want to die.

For three weeks I was in this panic. Then one day I sat down on a chair in my house. I am not sure whether I had a dream or a vision; I just know I got up from the chair and picked up my Bible and it opened at Psalm 23: "Even though I walk through the valley of the shadow of death ... your rod and your staff, they comfort me."[31] Those words spoke to my heart. He is with me. He will be my rod and staff.

Often when I was a young child walking alone down the road, the neighbours used to hit me on my head. But when I walked down the street with my father, nobody ever hit me or looked at me because I was with my father. Now, this verse in Psalm 23 told me I am holding Yeshua's hand and I am walking down the road with Him.

Then "N" was quiet. He was weeping.

They [the PA] executed one of my brothers. The other one left. He is no longer in the country. He had to escape; they were after him.

For five years now I have been ordered to attend the police station every Thursday. From morning to night they keep me there. They hit me. They put me in jail. They do this because I am a Christian.

I have a music degree and was a music teacher until one day the Ministry of Education called me to say the headmaster of the school where I taught had received complaints from parents to say I was destroying their children by persuading them to become Christians. "Why are you after me?" I asked them. "In Bethlehem and Ramallah there are teachers who are Muslims teaching music to children who are Christian."

The principal defended me. But some time later, while I was teaching at the school, I heard a message over the loudspeaker telling me to report to the principal. I went to his office to see why I had been called, only to find some members of the secret police there. They accused me of being a Christian, and a month later I received a letter telling me that I had lost my job and was forbidden to teach music at any school in the Palestinian Authority again.

Once again "N" fell silent – he was quietly weeping. We could hear the mullah's call to prayer from a nearby mosque. Traffic was rumbling past us. Life was going on all around us. But, I thought, what sort of a life do these people live here? To be a believer in Yeshua in the increasingly fundamentalist Islamic PA controlled areas of the West Bank was to live like a hunted animal. To be a believer in Yeshua in Ariel among religious Orthodox Jews who were prepared to leave a bomb on your doorstep with the intention of killing was equally shocking.

We were excommunicated in the village. They make fun of us because we are Christian. A week ago, my little son came home from school and he was crying. He said, "Father, I don't want to go back to school."

"What happened to you," I asked him.

"Everybody is calling me a Christian," he wept.

I didn't know what to do. I told him they were only small children and didn't know what they were saying. But he said, "No, no, no. You don't understand. The teacher was telling them what to say. She told me to leave the classroom because I was a Christian."

Now my son is having a lot of trouble at school.

More weeping.

This is the cost of living outside the camp, said David.

Even though this is happening, each time they come to destroy me, I am like a nail that is becoming more embedded inside the wood.

My wife had an operation for breast cancer yesterday. Nobody came to visit her from the village. The doctor had told the nurses, "Don't help this man and his wife. Don't give him pity. He's a Christian."

This is part of my life story. This is glory mixed with suffering – they walk together. They are planning to throw me out of the village soon. If they throw me out of the village – if they throw the pastor out of the village, what will happen to the sheep? I am praying I will stay in the village to care for the people who have become believers. There are four ladies who have really made a commitment recently.

We had been noticed; it was time to go. We prayed for "N" and he left.

While the vast majority of Palestinians living in the West Bank are Muslims, there are a significant number of Arabs living in Israel (known as Israeli Arabs) who are also Muslims. What is life like for them if they renounce their Muslim faith and become Christians?

I first met Kamel in Haifa in March 2013 shortly after he had entered the House of Victory (or Beit Nitzachon), a rehab centre for addicts run by believers.

I was born in Israel in a city called Shafar Aram. I come from a Muslim family, five brothers and three sisters. I am the eldest. One of my sisters drowned in the Sea of Galilee. My father is dead but my mother is still alive. I grew up doing what I wanted to do. I left school early because I wanted to. I never asked permission from anybody – I always did what I wanted to do. I was rebellious, especially against my father. I played football for many years. I married, but we later divorced. I wanted to escape the pain so I turned to drugs. Basically I became a heroin addict and my life took a different turn. I was arrested and sent to prison, and was then in and out of prison for many years. I became a drug dealer and made my living selling drugs. For thirty years I used and sold drugs. I spent many of those years in prison, and while there I tried to escape the habit by going on their rehab programmes. I also went to rehab out of prison – but nothing helped me.

Eventually I decided I wanted a fresh start. I could no longer live like this. My last time in prison was for six months and when I came out I knew I didn't want to go back. My friends at the time tried to persuade me to return to my old lifestyle, but I was determined to try to find a different way. I was drinking methadone, but I didn't want it any more. To get away from my "friends" I would go off by myself and find a quiet place and sit alone.

One Friday evening I was alone in a park next to the House of Victory when a guy called Khaled came up to me. I knew him – he was an Arab and we used to do drugs together. He told me he was staying at the House of Victory and he tried to persuade me to come. I told him it would be impossible for me to arrive unannounced but I asked him to talk to the boss and find out whether there was a place for me there. He readily agreed and told me to come back on Sunday. He also told me that the House of Victory was a House of God and God would help me to be healed from the power of drug addiction.

I stayed in that park next to the House of Victory. I was desperate for help and wanted to stay close to this House of God in the hope that Khaled would come and tell me there was a place for me there. When Sunday came, by 6 a.m. I was stood by the gate waiting to speak to the boss. Praise God, the door was opened to me and I was welcomed into the house by Eric Benson, the director.

I have suffered many things in my life and tried every possible way to try to be free from drugs. I have been here in the House of Victory for one year and it is a miracle that I am still here and free from the power of addiction. In my past life with drugs and dealing with drugs, there was no love or joy; I always felt I was living in darkness. But when I came to the House of Victory, I learned what love is. I learned what joy is. I experienced feeling relaxed and being calm and at peace. I no longer need to pretend with other people, I can talk to them humbly now and I know this is a gift to me from Yeshua. I can be myself now and talk to people nicely.

At the moment I am living day by day until I finish the programme.

Two years later, in February 2015, I met Kamel again. He looked well and was keen to bring me up to date with his story. He mentioned that when we had first met in 2013, he had only been drug free for a relatively short period and his memory then was poor. However, two years later and fully recovered, he could look back on his life and remember more details, particularly about his early years. Now aged fifty, although he was looking back on a life that had been ravaged by drug and alcohol abuse, he was, as you will read, also looking forward to what God has for him to do in the future. He reminded me that he was born into an Israeli Arab Muslim family and had five sisters and three brothers.

I went to school, but I never liked studying; I preferred football.

It started when I was growing up – there were a lot of problems at home. Everything that I liked to do I was forbidden to do. So many years of my life have been lost to drugs, alcohol, and time in prison.

However, I do thank the Lord that He has always surrounded me, and looking back I can see His hand of protection on my life. The night I saw Khaled in the park next to the House of Victory was the night that changed the course of my life. I had known him for a long time but that night I didn't recognize him at first: he had put some weight on and he looked so different and so well. When he told me his story and how he had found freedom from the power of addiction at the House of Victory, I knew that was where I wanted to go. I was so desperate to change my life and be healed from the curse of drug addiction. I thank the Lord that on that Sunday morning Eric Benson, the "boss", welcomed me into Beit Nitzachon (the Hebrew name for The House of Victory).

Although Beit Nitzachon welcomes both Jews and Arabs, it is a Messianic Jewish rehab centre. As he is from a Muslim background, I was interested to know Kamel's first impressions of stepping into an environment that would have been entirely new to him.

For the first few days I didn't realize who the other men in the house were and I didn't really understand the ethos of the house, that all the workers there were believers in Yeshua, Jesus; my main concern was that I wouldn't suffer too much pain from withdrawal from the drugs. Thankfully, the Lord Jesus worked quickly in my life. My eyesight had been affected by taking drugs for so long, and when I saw the other guys reading the Bible, I wanted to be able to do the same. So I asked

Eric to pray for me, that the Lord Jesus would heal my eyes, and then I began to read Psalm 51:

> Have mercy on me, O God,
> according to your unfailing love;
> according to your great compassion
> blot out my transgressions.
> Wash away all my iniquity
> and cleanse me from my sin.

Now I had one aim in life – to know the Lord Jesus. Very quickly I stopped thinking about Islam and concentrated on the Lord and how He was working in my life. When I read the Word of God, I knew it was working in me, changing me from the man I was to the man God made me to be. Now, every day when I wake up I am so thankful to know the Lord. Having Him in my life is priceless.

I am the only Christian in my family. I left home a long time ago. I was married and I have three sons but I have been far away from them for many years. Sometime after coming to the Lord, Eric was keen that I go and reconnect with my mother (my father had since died). I hadn't seen my mother or brothers and sisters for years. For some time I put it off, but after a year or more had passed, something inside started to tell me that I should go and see them. I mentioned this to Eric and we agreed that we would go the following morning. I filled a bag with Christian booklets, CDs, and magazines, and the next morning we set off together. We didn't phone to say we were coming; we just went not knowing what or who we would find.

I really wanted to see my mum. We arrived at the house and I knocked on the door. My mum opened the door and looked at me, she hugged me, and we cried. My brothers came and my sisters came. I didn't say a word. We just stood and gazed at each other, crying. One of my sisters said to me, "How did you get cleaned up?" Without hesitating I opened the bag and gave them the books and CDs. I also had a picture of the Lord Jesus in my bag. I took it and showed it to my family. Slowly and quietly I pointed at Him and said, "He is the one who got me cleaned up." We shared with them: it was a wonderful time.

Was it dangerous for me as a former Muslim to go back to my village as a believer in Jesus? As long as I am clean spiritually, and my heart and my life are clean, I am not afraid of anything or anybody. My mum came to Beit Nitzachon because she wanted to make sure that what had happened to me was real! She knelt down in the house and cried and thanked God for making me clean. It didn't matter to her that I had stopped being a Muslim and become a Christian; for her it was a matter that her son had got cleaned up after years and years and years. I was born and grew up in this country. Growing up I lived and played football with Jewish people. In Israel, we don't have the same political tensions as Palestinians living in the West Bank under Palestinian Authority control.

I thank the Lord for bringing me to faith. I know He is the Way, the Truth, and the Life. Everything is exposed. Everything is in the light. When my mum came to see where I live, she saw a picture of my

CHAPTER 4

Michael Kerem, a Jewish Missionary to the Muslim World

Gentile Christians sometimes find it difficult to understand the strong sense of "calling" or destiny experienced by many Jewish believers in Yeshua, particularly those who have left the country of their birth to go and live in Israel. Indeed, it can almost sound presumptuous (or even offensive) to Gentile ears when these same believers see themselves as a fulfilment of biblical prophecy and part of God's unfolding plan to be a blessing to all the nations of the earth.

What is the basis for such belief, and why do so many Gentile Christians find this offensive? Is it because they do not share a similar sense of purpose and destiny? If not, why not?

Michael Kerem is a softly spoken Israeli Jew originally from the United States. Together with his wife, Alev (who is Turkish), he has lived in Israel for many years. As you are about to discover, when Michael became a believer in Jesus as a young man, he immediately determined to live out, in practical ways, what he believes the Bible says about the days in which we live; that is, to play his part in the God-given calling of Israel to be a light to the nations, and in his case particularly to those nations that surround Israel. He firmly believes that God is working in an unprecedented manner in Israel and the Middle East and that biblical prophecy is being fulfilled. He is passionate about the relevance of the Bible and believes that for Christians to understand the conflict in the Middle East it is necessary to understand what the Scriptures have to say about the days in which we now live, both through the words of Jesus and through the Old Testament prophets.

He is particularly motivated by a prophecy in Isaiah which says:

> **In that day there will be a highway from Egypt to Assyria. The Assyrians will go to Egypt and the Egyptians to Assyria. The Egyptians and Assyrians will worship together. In that day Israel will be the third, along with Egypt and Assyria, a blessing on the earth. The Lord Almighty will bless them, saying, "Blessed be Egypt my people, Assyria my handiwork, and Israel my inheritance."**

Isaiah 19:23–25

Born into a secular Jewish family in San Francisco, Michael studied at Berkeley, California, and it was there the direction of his life changed course when he understood the calling of Yeshua on his life. Eager to prove that his faith would

74

work in the most challenging of situations, after graduating he left the comfort and security of the United States and turned his attention to the Muslim world.

Michael takes up the story …

After coming to faith just prior to university and while I was still there, I started to get interested in the Muslim world both because of its remoteness and because it is very intriguing, especially to me as a Jew. I felt there was still so much that was unknown about Islam and the Middle East. From my perspective, as a new believer and wanting to serve God, it looked like a vast empty space waiting to be discovered! As a young man I was also searching for adventure, and especially the opportunity to go to places where not many people from my background had travelled.

At graduate school there was a group of men who were teaching about Islam, and I found their lectures extremely interesting. I heard stories of people like Samuel Zwemer[32] who was one of the first people to go as a missionary from America to the Muslim world and send back reports of what he had seen. During the early twentieth century, when Zwemer was working in the Arabian Peninsula, the Middle East was starting to become of interest to the Western world because of the discovery of large quantities of oil.[33]

However, my heart was pulled to the Muslim world in the Middle East because they were among the most unreached of the unreached and I wanted to give my life in a place where nobody else was, and I wanted to test my faith in an area that would prove that if it didn't work there it wouldn't work anywhere. But that if it did work there it would work everywhere!

I found myself increasingly drawn to leave America and go to the Middle East as I began to appreciate that there was work I could do in taking the gospel to Muslim people. I was excited at the prospect of meeting the unknown and wanted to fulfil Jesus' command to, "Go into all the world and preach the good news to all creation."[34] Maybe that is something that is in every Jewish heart just as it was with Abraham when God said to him:

> "Leave your country, your people and your father's household and go to the land I will show you.
> I will make you into a great nation,
> and I will bless you;
> I will make your name great,
> and you will be a blessing.
> I will bless those who bless you,
> and whoever curses you I will curse;
> and all peoples on earth
> will be blessed through you."[35]

Leaving the States in the 1980s Michael travelled first to the Indian subcontinent and the islands of the Indian Ocean before arriving in Europe where he encountered Muslims living in the Western world. But it was the time he spent in Eastern Turkey that was to be the biggest influence in helping him to discover the destiny God had for his life.

While in Europe I met a man who came from the foot of Mount Ararat on the border with Russia, Armenia, and Eastern Turkey. He was Kurdish, and through talking to him and getting to know him I started to understand the history of the Kurdish people.

Many scholars believe the modern Kurdish people were known in ancient biblical times as the Medes, a people of Indo-Iranian origin who inhabited the western and north-western area of present-day Iran and Northern Iraq. It was the Medo-Persian armies, under the Persian conqueror Cyrus the Great, who in October 539 BC captured Babylon and brought to an end the Babylonian Empire. The Medo-Persian Empire, at its height, included 127 countries from Afghanistan and India in the east to southern Ethiopia and sub-Saharan Africa in the west.

From there I explored with other Kurdish friends the shared history between the Medes and the Jewish people during the Medo-Persian Empire, citing stories from the Bible describing this time; of how Daniel, in exile, became a trusted advisor to King Darius and how this kingdom was later ruled by Artaxerxes II who married Esther.

As well we discussed the link between the Medes' Zoroastrian faith and the Jewish faith (post-exilic) and how they influenced each other,[36] thus building another bridge of friendship and understanding between us which was to help me later as a Jewish person working among the Kurdish people. It both surprised and delighted me that they were interested and knew so much about my heritage, and this in turn provoked me to learn a lot more about the link between the ancient Jewish people and the Kurds.

Working among Muslim people in the countries of the Middle East, Michael had no intention of ever going to live in Israel. However, all that was to change.

We did not plan to come and live here originally. My wife, Alev, is Turkish. We met in Turkey while working on a mission team. At first, communication was difficult between us because I didn't speak Turkish and Alev didn't speak English! I actually proposed to her through an interpreter! After we married we thought we would be moving to a country further east of Turkey. Coming to live in Israel, even as a Jew, was not something I was planning. Many Jewish people from North America say they will retire to Israel – one day – perhaps! So for us to come and live in Israel and use this as our base to go to the Muslim world was unexpected. However, it became a practical issue because we were searching for a place where we could raise our family while working in and travelling around the Middle East; we didn't actually come initially for theological or prophetic reasons!

It was only later that we realized how significant it was that we were living in Israel at this time. Sometimes it is only with hindsight that we can understand the will of God and appreciate why we do certain things at particular times. Abraham left Ur not knowing where he was going. And when we came here to Jerusalem, we actually didn't know the full reasons as to why God had brought us here.

God began to unfold that to us gradually, and as we studied the Bible, in particular the Old Testament, we realized why the Jewish people are being called back to the land of Israel from nations all over the world where they have been living for centuries. They are not called just to inherit a land and be blessed. Rather they are called, ultimately, to bless all the nations of the earth. For us, given the work we were doing, that meant the nations surrounding Israel.

When we came to live in Israel, we began to understand the strategic importance of being here as sons of Isaac living among the sons of Ishmael, and to realize that not only was our history connected but also our destiny.

We were keen to understand the bigger picture as to what God is doing in Israel and the wider Middle East at this time. What is the role of Israel in God's plan? What should we Jewish believers be doing?

For many Christians, reading Paul's letter to the Romans can be perplexing. We understand the first eight chapters but then wonder why he appears to take a detour during chapters 9 to 11 to talk about Israel and the Jewish people before returning to his original theme. But in my opinion, a careful reading of Romans shows a strong and consistent direction, and in chapters 9 to 11 Paul concludes his argument as he explains that God's plan is to bring the Jewish people back into God's covenant promises and purposes. He says, "God's gifts and his call are irrevocable."[37] This means that even if the Jewish people are not walking in their redemption they are still going to influence nations for better or for worse, in every sphere of life, whether in the media, the arts, finance, the legal world, the medical world, and even in the spiritual world. So, we must conclude, their calling (and this is God's choice, not ours) is to be a blessing to the nations. Whether they walk in it redemptively or not, they will influence nations.

As always, questions regarding biblical prophecy are many and various. Isaiah the prophet lived in Jerusalem approximately 2,700 years ago, and it was during his lifetime that the Assyrian Empire conquered the northern part of Israel. Isaiah wrote many detailed prophecies about the first coming of the Messiah, and we know this happened 700 years later with the birth of Jesus. Today, we can look back and see that many of Isaiah's prophecies have been fulfilled.[38]

I have observed an increasing number of Messianic Jewish believers and Arab Christians talking about the prophecy found in Isaiah 19:23–25.

For Michael and Alev Kerem, this passage carries particular significance given the work they are involved with in sharing the gospel with Muslim people in the nations that surround Israel; the nations mentioned in these verses. Non-Hebrew speakers would generally interpret the word "highway" as being a major road. But what does it mean in Hebrew?

The Hebrew word used by Isaiah, translated "highway" in English, is "mesillah". This is a very unusual word and means a road that is exalted above the nations.

Today Egypt is a very influential nation in the Middle East, especially for the Muslim world. In the earlier part of Isaiah 19, the message to Egypt describes a shaking, then a striking, followed by healing and their redemption. Then Isaiah sees a highway from Egypt to Assyria which includes Israel. When Isaiah wrote this prophecy, the situation then was similar to the situation in the Middle East today. Why do I say that? All relationships in the Middle East are defined by one simple principle that is practised by people and governments: "The enemy of my enemy is my friend."[39]

People form alliances in the Middle East based around a common enemy. An example of this happened recently when one of Saudi Arabia's leaders talked about Israel using its airspace to attack Iran. Who would have thought that Saudi Arabia and Israel would cooperate together? But why were they together? They were together around a common alliance over someone they did not like or trust.

But the Isaiah 19 highway is different because this is an alliance based not on who you are against. Rather it is based on who you are for. It is based on worshipping the sovereign Lord. And this is very unusual because not only is it based on worship, but it is also based on enemies worshipping together.

In the time of Isaiah, Assyria was the dominant kingdom of its period and it was bearing down on Israel. The leaders of Israel had a choice. Should they make an alliance with Egypt, their enemy, against their greater enemy Assyria, or should they pay tribute to Assyria in order to subdue Egypt? The dynamics of that time are the same today – who does Israel align with against its enemies?

Isaiah's response must have surprised everybody when he prophesied about a coming highway between Egypt and Assyria that included Israel. This route is similar to the road Abraham took when he left his home in Haran (in Assyria) and travelled through the land of Israel all the way to Egypt before eventually returning back to settle in Israel.

As we started to study this chapter, our attention was particularly drawn to the part of Isaiah's prophecy that speaks about nations worshipping together and being a blessing on the earth. We began to realize there was something here that was above and beyond what we had ever thought of or indeed could have ever imagined. Nowhere else in the Bible does it talk about "Egypt my people" or the brutal and oppressive kingdom of Assyria as "my handiwork".

It rang a chord in our spirits that reminded us that God is sovereign over the nations. This prophecy describes something He is doing that we could never have imagined.

We took these verses in Isaiah 19 as our guide. We were based here in Israel, yet we were to go out to the nations. You can imagine when a Jewish believer in Yeshua from Israel arrives in a remote Muslim village in the middle of Turkey, or Iraq, or Egypt and starts to speak about his faith in Yeshua, it attracts some attention! However, we do not publicize what we do, and most of what we do is done on a very small scale – on a one-to-one, house-to-house basis.

It is not easy for us to go to these Muslim villages, but when we speak to the people about Jesus they are so thankful to meet us. They say to us, "You are Jewish, yet you believe in Yeshua. I'm a son of Ishmael. I may be a Muslim, but I can believe in Yeshua too!" They say, "You've done this so I can do it too!"

The Middle East is very much defined by what we call the status quo; in other words, what you are born defines what or who you are and you cannot change that in order to be anything else. So a Jew is born a Jew and must die a Jew. The Muslim is born a Muslim and must die a Muslim. So when you meet somebody who has actually broken the status quo, then you start to think, "Wait a minute – I can do that too." We watch as people realize they can step outside of the culture or religion they were born into, although it may be costly. The highway described in Isaiah 19 does just that. It steps outside of the status quo and describes enemies coming together to be a blessing, doing something that nobody could have imagined possible.

Today we are witnessing many Muslim people becoming believers in the Messiah, Jesus. Twenty years ago I don't think we would have believed what we have begun to see today. It has nothing to do with us. This is happening as the result of thousands of Christians around the world praying for the Muslim people. In 1994 there was an initiative called "Praying through the 10/40 window" which ignited and mobilized prayer for both the Muslim and Jewish people in the Middle East.[40]

The changes we have seen in the past twenty years, whether in Iran, Jordan, Iraq, or Egypt, have meant we have seen more Muslims and more Jewish people coming to faith in Yeshua than in the whole of history. In addition, I see that not only are they coming to faith; they are also wanting to build relationships with those "on the other side". In other words, when a Muslim comes to faith, he wants to meet with Jewish believers, the sons of Isaac. He wants to come and see where they live. Similarly, when Jews come to faith in Yeshua, they are increasingly starting to realize they are not here in the Middle East just to take ownership of this little piece of ground called Israel. Rather, they realize the purpose for them being in Israel is to invite "Ishmael" back into the house. He was rejected but now we need to bring him back. We know of Jewish believers who are learning Arabic and other languages because they want to be a part of God's answer for the Middle East and not the problem.

Are we seeing this movement increasing? Twenty years ago, when we first came to this nation of Israel as immigrants, we were definitely very unusual. At that time there were very few Jewish believers in Jesus and people didn't know what to think of us. But today, our numbers have grown and we are better understood.

Increasingly, Messianic believers are thinking and talking about reaching people in other nations. Indeed, they are believing that God is going to use them to go to other nations. We are not the only people involved in this Isaiah 19 movement. There are many expressions. Young people are coming together, along with people from many nations, to pray about these verses in Isaiah 19 concerning the highway. They have a common desire to understand the significance of praying about this particular prophecy at this time. Others are getting involved with initiatives to do with mercy and relief to help alleviate the suffering in the nations surrounding Israel. There is currently an initiative to bring Israeli, Egyptian, Turkish, and Kurdish believers together into a discipleship school where they can all learn and study the Bible together in a secure place and community. On the one hand we are seeing the Arab nations being shaken. On the other hand we are seeing unprecedented opportunities.

I had really good theological training when I was growing up, not because I sought it out but because I happened to be in a place where there were teachers who helped me to understand what the kingdom of God is. I learned that the kingdom of God is not the church and the church is not the kingdom. The kingdom of God is much more expansive. In fact, Yeshua only made reference to the church once, while He made reference to the kingdom of God approximately eighty times.

Understanding what the kingdom of God is got me very excited because it gave me a framework not only to understand the parables of Jesus; it also helped me to understand the prophetic Scriptures. And really, the prophetic is the future invading the present. I do not know how fast what is coming at us is coming. I don't think that those of us who have lived and worked in the Middle East for the past twenty or thirty years believed that we would see the things we are seeing today.

But it is my prayer, and I don't think it is too far off, that when we look at those words in Isaiah 19 where he says, "In that day," we are beginning to see something of the future happening now. In other words, I believe, "In that day," is already starting to happen now. It is only a taste, a foreshadowing, but it is beginning to happen. Where we are on the timeline I don't know. One thing I have learned is to expect the unexpected.

After living in the Middle East for the past thirty years and experiencing a great deal of trouble, division, and conflict, not only between nations but also among believing colleagues, I have begun to understand an important principle in interpersonal relationships: the number one reason why Christian workers leave the mission field is because God does not give us grace for the offence of another. In other words, if I did something to you, God would give you grace to forgive me. But if you told a friend about this, God would not give your friend grace to forgive me because I did not hurt your friend. This describes what many Christians do in the Middle East. They tend to take on the offences of one side or the other. Jesus said very clearly that if we want to walk in the kingdom, we have to learn to forgive just as His Father in heaven forgives us.[41] So it is really important that we guard our hearts.

It is important that we base our prayers and our vision of the Middle East on God's purposes, His covenant, and His promises, and not on what we read in the news. In other words, the situation in the Middle East is much wider and bigger than the Palestinian/Israeli conflict. God's purposes are much greater than the conflict here because His plan is to bring His kingdom to all the people living in the Middle East. I believe Isaiah 19 really expresses that, along with many other prophetic Scriptures.

The other thing that can sometimes be hard for people to understand is that over 50 per cent of the prophetic Scriptures relate to one central event – the return of the Jewish people to their ancient homeland. Isaiah 19 could not happen without the Jewish people being here. I cannot comment on the borders specifically, but I do know that it is important the Jews are back here because God wants to use them in His purposes regarding the sons of Ishmael.

So far we had been considering the situation regarding the nations surrounding Israel in the context of Isaiah 19 and the highway, or Abrahamic path, mentioned there. But what about the rest of the world? Do Christians living in nations outside the Middle East have any part to play in these events?

Not only is the attention of the world's media constantly on Jerusalem, but the numbers of Christians coming here these days is unprecedented, and they are coming with an expectation to understand what is coming upon the world and ask what season are we about to enter. The prophet Zechariah said,

"And many peoples and powerful nations will
come to Jerusalem to seek the Lord Almighty and
to entreat him ... In those days ten men from all
languages and nations will take firm hold of one Jew
by the hem of his robe and say, 'Let us go with you,
because we have heard that God is with you.'"[42]

There are a number of different gatherings that are
going to happen in the near future in Jerusalem where
Muslim-background believers and Asian believers
from many powerful nations are going to come to
worship the Lord in Jerusalem. My prayer is that some
of these gatherings will start to draw the attention of
not only the secular community but also the religious
community here in Israel so that they start to enquire
as to what is happening. What is all this interest? Why
all this outpouring of love and adoration not only for
the God of Israel, Abraham, Isaac, and Jacob, but also
for the Jewish people?

I am living in Jerusalem where the number of Jewish
believers is still relatively small. There are also a number
of Arab and Palestinian Christians that we are closely
involved with. As you might expect, there are deep
tensions between us that we are determined will not
divide us. With so many people coming to Jerusalem
from the nations to meet us, is it going to be a big
challenge? Yes! But we are used to being the smallest
tribe from among the smallest and most rejected
people! It's my understanding of the Scriptures that
most of the things God does are counter-intuitive;
they don't fit with our natural way of thinking. The
issue of humility is not so much thinking you are the

least; it's more accepting your place regardless of whatever everybody else says about you, regardless of your physical numbers, and regardless of your physical appearance. So we are going to have to move away from our inferiority complex as a body and we (both the Messianic Jewish community and the Arab/Palestinian Christian community) are going to have face the challenge of how we can walk together so that we can bless all the nations of the earth rather than take their attention and let them feel sorry for us. So we are going to have to move beyond our victimization, our smallness, and our feelings of inferiority and instead embrace God's prophetic words about us being a blessing (Isaiah 19) to all the nations of the earth.

So what are the most important passages of Scripture that people should be looking at today if they want to understand what God is doing, not just here in Jerusalem but in the world?

It has been my understanding from reading the gospels that Yeshua often quoted from Isaiah. As already mentioned, over 50 per cent of biblical prophecy about God's dealings with the nations has to do with the matter of the restoration of the Jewish people to their ancient homeland of Israel. This is still going on today.

But more than that, I believe it is important to look carefully at the connections with our neighbours – the nations surrounding Israel. I am convinced that in the coming days God will increasingly use Jewish believers to bring the Muslim people to faith in Yeshua.

On the other hand, we are expecting more than fifty Muslim-background believers to come here to Jerusalem in the near future; these are people who are passionate about meeting with their Messianic Jewish brothers. This is a prophetic sign, like a first fruit, showing what God is doing to get the attention of the nation of Israel. In his letter to the Romans, Paul put it like this:

> for I want somehow to make the people of Israel
> jealous of what you Gentiles have, so I might save
> some of them.[43]

Already we are seeing how God is using the stories of MBBs coming to Jerusalem to cause questions to arise in the minds of Jewish people (both secular and religious). We are noticing that they are starting to enquire as to how it can be possible for a former Muslim to embrace the God of Israel and believe that Jesus is the (Jewish) Messiah. These MBBs are beginning to stir the "jealousy" referred to in the above verse!

The world is so used to the conflict between Isaac and Ishmael so what will be the reaction when they witness a restoration to the Father and to each other?

CHAPTER 5

Andrey Teplinsky – a Russian Jew in Israel

I t takes only a brief glimpse into the history of the Jewish people over the past 2,000 years to see how anti-Semitism has surfaced frequently around the world and cost millions of Jewish lives. They have endured pogroms, mob attacks, expulsion, public torture and execution, forced conversions and mass murders, massacres, and the Holocaust, yet they have survived as a people. Not only that, in recent times thousands have left the nations to which they were dispersed and returned to live in their ancient homeland of Israel.

As already mentioned in chapter four, over 50 per cent of the prophetic Scriptures relate to the return of the Jewish people to their ancient homeland. This is exactly what has happened in recent history and is still happening today. Their individual stories are many and varied, but when placed side by side a clear thread emerges as people describe being drawn as though by an invisible cord, a creeping awareness that they would be better in Israel than remaining where they are.

This movement has often been prompted by trouble, making it impossible for Jewish people to remain living in their "adopted" country. Jews living in France have been unsettled by the rise in anti-Semitism there, most recently by the murder of four people in a Jewish supermarket in Paris on Friday 7 January 2015 following the killing of twelve journalists at the *Charlie Hebdo* offices. Stephen Pollard, editor of the *Jewish Chronicle*, reported in the *Daily Telegraph* on 9 January 2015:

> **The least surprising thing about today's turn of events in Paris is that Jews are the target. Because when it comes to home grown anti-Semitism, France leads the world.**
>
> **A survey last year from the European Jewish Congress and Tel Aviv University found that France had more violent anti-Semitic incidents in 2013 than any other country in the world. Jews were the target of 40 per cent of all racist crimes in France in 2013 – even though they comprise less than 1 per cent of the population. Attacks on Jews have risen sevenfold since the 1990s.**
>
> **No wonder Jewish emigration from France is accelerating. From being the largest Jewish community in the European Union at the start of this decade, with a population of around 500,000, it is expected by Jewish community leaders to have fallen to 400,000 within a few years. That figure is thought by some to be too optimistic. Anecdotally, every French Jew I know**

**has either already left or is working out how to
leave.**

**Natan Sharansky, the former Soviet refusenik
who is now chair of the Jewish Agency, said
last year that 2,254 French Jews moved to Israel
during the first five months of 2014, against only
580 in all of 2013. That is a staggering 289 per
cent increase, but in recent months the figure is
thought to have increased exponentially.**

However, it is Jews from the former Soviet Union who have
formed the largest group immigrating to Israel. When, in
1989, the Soviet Premier Mikhail Gorbachev decided to lift
restrictions on Russians who wanted to leave the country,
more than 12,000 Jews immediately immigrated to Israel.
In 1990, a further 183,400 Soviet Jews made aliyah to Israel,
followed by 148,000 in 1991. Between 1992 and 1995, on
average 70,000 Jews per year immigrated to Israel from the
former Soviet Union, and still they are arriving.

In 1998, aged twenty-three, a Russian Jew called
Andrey Teplinsky decided to move to Israel.

His life began in Birobidzhan, a region in the southern
part of the former Soviet Far East on the border with
Manchuria. On 28 March 1928, the General Executive
Committee of the Soviet Union (under Joseph Stalin)
approved the establishment of a Jewish national region and
Birobidzhan was chosen. Jewish people were encouraged
to relocate, and between 1928 and 1938 approximately
43,000 Jews moved there, including Andrey's grandparents
(his father's parents). Covering an area of 34,000 square

kilometres, the region is comparable in size to the Netherlands or Taiwan.

At that time Stalin was keen to encourage the development of the various national identities that made up the Russian population, and the Jewish people were considered one such group.

The Kremlin had three reasons for establishing Birobidzhan as a Jewish settlement. Firstly to redirect the movement of Jews to the land away from Ukraine, Belarus, and Crimea where the local population was strongly resistant to any Jewish settlement. Secondly to provide a buffer zone for the Soviet Union from Chinese and Japanese expansionism. And thirdly to use the Jews as a workforce to tap the natural resources of fish, tin, iron, timber, gold, and graphite that were plentiful in the region. Until then, most of the 2.5 million Jews living in Russia had lived in small towns and cities and eked out a meagre living. In Birobidzhan they hoped for a better life, although when they arrived, they discovered they were not alone: 27,000 Russians, Cossacks, Koreans, and Ukrainians were already living in the region.

Andrey's father was born in Birobidzhan in 1943 during the Second World War. He met his wife there and in 1969 their first child, a boy, was born. Andrey was born in 1974.

I met Andrey in March 2015 and he shared his moving account of how and why he left his family in Russia and came alone to live in Israel. Little did he realize the problems he would face, yet his story illustrates the inner calling within the Jewish heart to live in Israel.

We grew up under a communist regime and the ideology of there being no God. At home my parents never spoke about God and we didn't follow any Jewish traditions, but my auntie sometimes cooked Jewish food for us and occasionally she spoke briefly about the Jewish holidays and feasts.

My brother and I went to a school where most of the teachers were Jewish.

When I was sixteen I had to apply for an identity card. I remember going to the government office and when asked what my nationality was I immediately replied, "Russian," because I was already weary of being identified as Jewish and therefore considered different. I wanted to be the same as everybody else.

The collapse of the Soviet Union was heralded on 25 December 1991 when the hammer and sickle flag was lowered for the last time over the Kremlin. The president, Mikhail Gorbachev, resigned and Boris Yeltsin became president of the newly independent Russian state. In 1990, before Mikhail Gorbachev resigned, his government had allowed the borders of the former Soviet Republic to open, thus allowing Jews to leave and go to Israel.

I was sixteen years old when the Soviet Union collapsed. When I heard about the thousands of Jewish people who were leaving Russia to make aliyah (immigrate) to Israel, my world view started to change. Entire families were packing up and leaving; it was a phenomenal time of upheaval. Sometimes my father would jokingly suggest that one day perhaps we too would move to Israel. But our lives carried on as before, and two years later I went to university and began my studies in history and English language.

One morning I left our house as usual and went to the university, but when I returned home in the afternoon, just five hours later, the house was full of people and my mother was crying. My father had died. He was only forty-nine years old. I could not believe it because I had only seen him that morning and he had seemed absolutely normal; I had noticed nothing in his behaviour to suggest that anything was wrong with him. I was so shocked it took me two or three days to realize my father had passed away and I would never see or talk to him again.

Unable to concentrate, and losing all enthusiasm for study, I left the university. I had lost the person who had guided me through life and now I found myself alone. The sadness and sense of loss was so great that I opened the door of my life to other things to try and dull the pain, and one of those things was drugs.

My life became so empty and the addiction to drugs so strong. If I was going to survive, I knew I had to get away and try and rebuild my life. Four years after losing my father I decided that now was the time to make a choice about leaving Russia and moving to Israel. I reasoned with myself that because I was Jewish, I was entitled to make aliyah to Israel. How could I be refused entry?

When I told my mother and brother that I was planning to move to Israel they thought I was joking because they could not believe I had the strength or courage to take such a big step. However, I was determined. I went to the Israeli Embassy and completed all the paperwork and supplied them with all the relevant documents to prove my Jewish credentials. Eventually I heard that my application had been accepted, told the date I would be leaving, and given a ticket to fly to Israel.

It was only when my mother and brother saw me packing my bags that they realized I was actually about to leave. It was 1998. I was twenty-three years old.

What I really wanted to do was change myself because my addiction to drugs had turned into a nightmare. I realized that I was thinking about drugs all the time. I hoped that if I could change my environment I could also change my lifestyle and leave my bad habits.

However, in reality I was wrong!

I arrived in Israel in the month of August and was immediately sent to an absorption centre for new immigrants in the city of Tiberias situated on the western shores of the Sea of Galilee. The month of August in Tiberias is the hottest place in Israel! I thought I would die there! And so I found myself in a different country, speaking a different language, surrounded by different people – but the same me!

Shortly after arriving in Tiberias I met some people who also used drugs, and before long my new life in Israel, which had been so full of hope, turned into a nightmare because drugs were readily available and very easy to buy. I started to commit crimes in order to support this habit and eventually I was arrested for stealing and sent to prison. During my first seven years in Israel I spent almost five years in and out of prison. I was alone and desperate to know how to change my life.

While still in prison I met a person who told me about a rehabilitation centre for drug addicts and alcoholics in Haifa called the House of Victory (Beit Nitzachon). He also told me they were believers in Yeshua (Jesus) and suggested I made contact with them. I wasn't particularly keen on this idea because for me, being a Jewish person, I imagined that a centre run by Christians would be like living in a monastery, and I did not want to become a monk!

However, when I was released from prison I decided that perhaps I should go to Haifa to meet people at the House of Victory. I was alone in the world and knew how vulnerable I was to falling back into drug addiction and a life of crime. Five years in prison had been a very long time and I did not want to return there.

My first impression on entering the House of Victory was how normal it looked. I couldn't see any crosses or other Christian religious symbols and so I decided that maybe these people could help me after all.

However, the first week was challenging on a personal level because I smoked cigarettes, and one of the rules at the House of Victory is that smoking is forbidden. It was not easy for me to accept the fact that if I was to stay in the programme I would have to give up smoking. At the same time, I realized that I needed to stay if I really wanted to change my lifestyle and be free from addiction to drugs.

The second problem I encountered right from the start was the way the days were organized. The daily routine required me to study the Bible, spend time singing hymns, and help with the housework and cooking. I found myself in an environment where there was an invisible God who, I was told, would help me to change my life. In return I had to be prepared to take certain steps, and the first step was I had to believe in Him! Coming from a background where I had been taught that God did not exist, this was not easy, and during my first month at the House of Victory I fought a personal battle between faith and disbelief. Could I really believe there was a God who could change my life?

Gradually, with encouragement from the staff and the other men, I started to read the Bible. One morning as I was reading a psalm I was surprised to find myself crying. It was as though that psalm was all about my life and I realized that the message of hope it contained was for me. For the first time in my life I felt that God was real and that He had been waiting for me to turn to Him for years. This awareness of the truth started to liberate my mind from thoughts of drugs; addiction began to lose its hold on me. I knew I was changing. As I gained an understanding of who God is, I started to realize who I am in His sight.

The first miracle I received was a revelation that God is my Father. This truth started to liberate my mind, and as I studied the Word of God I saw on every page of the Bible that God has an everlasting love for every individual. I wanted to know about His love for me. I stopped thinking about drugs and cigarettes and found myself concentrating on the love of God towards me. I started to spend time with God alone in prayer. I would sit and read the Word of God and pray and ask God to touch me and heal me. After a while I realized I was different. It was experiencing the love of God that released me from the power of drugs.

Today Andrey is married, he is writing books, he is a teacher in the congregation he attends, and he has a strong sense of destiny.

As I studied the Bible I began to realize that we are living in very interesting times because, through biblical prophets such as Jeremiah and Ezekiel, God promised to bring His ancient people, the Jews, back to the land He had promised to Abraham, Isaac, and Jacob, and He promised to give them a new heart and a new spirit.

For example, I read in the book of the prophet Ezekiel:

> "For I will take you out of the nations; I will gather you from all the countries and bring you back into your own land. I will sprinkle clean water on you, and you will be clean; I will cleanse you from all your impurities and from all your idols. I will give you a new heart and put a new spirit in you. I will remove from you your heart of stone and give you a heart of flesh. And I will put my Spirit in you and move you to follow my decrees and be careful to keep my laws. You will live in the land I gave your forefathers; you will be my people, and I will be your God."[44]

When I read these and other similar prophetic verses in the Bible, I realized that I, a Jew, had come to live in the land of my forefathers and I had received a new heart and a new spirit when I started to believe in Yeshua, the Messiah. As the realization dawned on me that I was a part of prophecy being fulfilled, so I began to understand that God had a specific destiny for my life.

Today I am serving in a Messianic congregation on Mount Carmel called Kehilat H'Carmel where my "job description" is teaching and praying. I teach the classes for new believers; a team of us are regularly out on the streets of Haifa sharing our faith, and the people who are coming to the Lord come to my classes. I am teaching them how to simply live with God, how to hear His voice, how to understand His Word, and how to move from being an enemy of God to being a child of God.

I am also involved in prayer and intercession because it is clear from the Bible that God is waiting for a voice of faith from the earth, a voice that God will answer. The heavens and God Himself are waiting to hear people proclaim God's promises for the Jewish people. Hence there is a need for intercession. I find that part of my spiritual destiny in the Lord is to stand in the gap for my people at this time. From my own experience of having my life transformed, I understand that it is possible for anybody, no matter what their life has been like in the past, to make the transition from being in a place of darkness and despair to a place of hope and purpose, and to become a blessing for our nation; a person who is reminding God about His promises for His people. And when I see how God is answering our prayers, as we are seeing more people coming to the Lord, I am happy!

Andrey is a man who, because of his own story and experience, sees his life story written into the pages of the Bible; for him the Bible has and is coming alive before his eyes as he is seeing, quite literally, biblical prophecy being fulfilled. Indeed, he sees himself as part of the fulfilment of biblical prophecy. What does it do to you when, along with others, you experience that level of revelation and realize you are part of this great movement?

First of all, when I meet others who are also walking in this same understanding of the Word of God and appreciate the times in which we are living, it creates a sense of unity and family. It is very encouraging that, in this battle for Jewish hearts, I am not alone. Together we understand that God has a family in the land of Israel, and we are like an army. What I like is that when we are together doing outreaches, or praying together and interceding for the Jewish nation, I understand that what God is doing in our midst, He wants to do throughout the nation. I see myself as being a part of this saved remnant and I believe that what God has done for me, He wants to do for every Jewish person who lives in Israel. So I am very excited to see where I am and what I am doing!

I believe that what God is doing here in Israel today should matter to Christians living in the rest of the world because the restoration of the modern

State of Israel in May 1948 was a historical event, and for all of us who are believers in Yeshua, Jesus, it has a prophetic significance as well. Never before in the history of the world has a people been regathered to their homeland after being dispersed around the world for 2,000 years. Today everybody can see the vast numbers of Jewish people from around the world who have come to live here. As believers looking at this we see that the invisible hand of God has brought His people back to live in Israel. The same God who scattered His people 2,000 years ago is regathering them, and nobody can stop what is happening.

Secondly, the fact that the Jewish people are back in the land of Israel is a sign for us that Jesus is coming back soon. Jewish people are building their houses, Israel has become a nation that leads the world in so many areas including medicine and technology, but what is of most significance to us believers is that God is preparing His ancient people for the return of His Son. This is our hope. We are longing for His appearance. The nation of Israel today is a sign to every individual in the world that there is a God, He is real, and He is about to do something that everybody will see – the return of His Son to His own land.

I am a member of a congregation that embraces Arab Christians as well as Jewish believers. At first this was a challenge because for me as a Jewish immigrant, it was not easy to readily love the Arab people because through human eyes they look like troublemakers. But in reality they are not. I have Arab believers and unbelievers as my friends. In the community that I am part of we have Jews and non-Jews living together. In fact, my wife is not Jewish: she is from Spain. Now I find it exciting that I have Arab friends who are a part of our congregation. When we (Jews and Arabs) receive the Lord, He starts to work in our hearts and we experience Him pulling down the walls that have separated us and showing us that through the cross, in Yeshua the Messiah, we are one, we are equal, and our ethnicity does not matter. We are all children of God whether we are a Jew from the former Soviet Union or an Arab from the land of Israel: in Yeshua we are all equal and loved in God's sight. This changing of attitudes is supernatural; it is a miracle. But it is happening more and more. To be part of a congregation where "enemies" have become brothers is so beautiful.

I have come a long way in my life, but I know there is still more to experience as the Lord goes on transforming us and revealing the Scriptures to us and helping us to understand His unfolding plan of salvation for the world.

CHAPTER 6

Magdy and Rima Anwar – an Egyptian Pastor in Jerusalem

I first met Magdy and Rima Anwar in Switzerland at a celebratory event for a couple who had been involved in mission work in the Middle East for twenty-five years. They were mutual friends of ours and it just so happened that my husband and I were sat at the same table as Magdy and Rima.

My first impression of them was how quiet and self-effacing they were. It was only later when they shared, albeit reluctantly, a little of their background that I recognized that here was a couple with a most unusual story.

Just before leaving, we exchanged email addresses. Then Magdy and Rima returned to Jerusalem and we returned to the UK, but not before they had invited us to visit them when next in Israel.

I kept their contact details safe and when this book started to emerge in my mind, of stories about people God appears to be using to fulfil His plans in Israel in these days, their names had to be on the list.

But would they be willing to share the details of their lives? You will not find anything about Magdy and Rima Anwar on the internet. No book has been written about this couple. No film made about their lives. To date they have remained invisible, out of sight. Why?

Throughout history there will have been countless people that we will never know about and who will remain unknown to us because, although they achieved much in God's sight, their work was never recognized or recorded as being significant in the world's eyes. Their memories and their stories died with them.

Magdy and Rima Anwar have that same attitude. As with all the people whose stories are included in this book, celebrity status will never trouble them in this world! However, when looking at these people through God's eyes, we see them in a different light. Hear their stories and you realize you are in the presence of people God has handpicked for His work.

In chapter three of this book, we looked at the lives of three men who were born into the Muslim culture. Their identity was Muslim. As far as their families and their communities were concerned, they were born Muslim and they would die Muslim. However, we saw what happened to them, especially those coming from a fundamentalist Muslim background in the West Bank, when they chose to change their Muslim identity and "put on" a Christian identity. Their lives were immediately in danger and they were forced to live like hunted animals.

So who is going to care for such people? If, as it would appear, judging by the increasing number of stories that are emerging, vast numbers of people are going to be changing their identity from Muslim to Christian in the coming months and years, what fate awaits them? Who can they turn to for advice and support?

When I returned to Jerusalem early in 2015 to continue the research for this book, I visited Magdy and Rima in their rented apartment in Jerusalem. My first impression of entering their home was one of hospitality! The table was overflowing with fruit and nuts, cakes, and drinks. Outside the weather was cold and wet. But inside, with the electric radiators on full power, the room was warm and welcoming. They have tried their hardest to create a place they can call home when, in fact, home for each of them is in a different country. For Magdy, home is in Egypt. And for Rima, home is in Jordan. So what are they doing in Jerusalem? Magdy began to share his story.

I was raised in a Coptic Christian family in Egypt. My mother was a believer and I watched her having her quiet time every day. I heard her praying for my dad and our family; there were six of us children – three boys and three girls. Even as a young child I recognized that she had a special intimacy with God, and when I was young I often woke up to hear her singing. So I began to sit close beside her and imitate what she was doing. I suppose I wanted what she had!

As I grew older I started to ask myself, "What is a true Christian?" I regularly attended the Coptic Orthodox church. I memorized verses of Scripture and some prayers and tried to pray like my mum did. But however hard I tried, I did not experience the same intimacy with God that my mother enjoyed. Can it be that I am trying by my own efforts? Is there something missing? What is a true Christian? How can I find that intimacy with God that my mother experiences? These questions kept going round and round in my mind.

When I was sixteen years old, a man came to our home. He spoke about David and how he had sinned (with Bathsheba). He then described David's heartfelt prayer of repentance to God, asking for forgiveness for what he had done. I interrupted him: "Wait a minute, I have a question. If you can answer it, then I will listen to what you have to say. What does it mean to be a true Christian? I memorize verses, I read the Bible, I have a quiet time like my mum, I go to the church; what else do I have to do in order to be a true Christian?"

He looked at me and smiled. "You're doing a great job," he said, "but there is one more thing you need to do: ask the Lord to come into your heart."

And so I did. With all my heart I asked Jesus to come into my life because I was desperate to have this intimacy with Jesus like my mum.

For two weeks nothing happened. Then, one day, I found myself singing a song. It was a song that I had sung many times before, but now I kept singing it! Everything had changed. I was talking to "someone". Tears flowed from my eyes as I started to experience an intimacy in my relationship with Jesus. One morning, as I was in the room where I usually went for my quiet time, I opened the Bible and started to read as usual, but this time it was different; it was as though someone was talking to me! So, in 1973, when I was sixteen years old, I began to discover a relationship with Jesus just like my mum.

I finished my education at High School in Alexandria and started to help organize a youth meeting at the church. My life carried on and I went to college. But all the while I had a deep desire to be in the ministry and work for the Lord full-time.

When I was twenty-seven years old and just about to complete my studies, I was invited to join a training programme in evangelism and discipleship. This raised many questions in my mind. In my heart I didn't just want to go on training programmes. I was about to leave college and had been studying for years! Rather I wanted to be in the ministry working among people. However, I agreed to join their programme. It was November 1985.

A month later, in December, I attended a large international training conference on evangelism. This had a profound effect on my life as I realized that evangelism was what I wanted to do more than anything else. I approached the organization who had hosted the conference and asked if I could work in the ministry with them. To my delight they agreed.

My work started in Alexandria, then expanded to include Cairo and then the whole of Egypt. I was leading a training programme teaching groups of Christians in churches throughout Egypt how to reach the people in their communities with the gospel. I was excited. I enjoyed training people. I liked taking people from A to B and from B to C so they could develop and help their churches to expand.

At the same time, I felt lonely and had a deep desire to find a wife and get married! Not only was I lonely, but I was also visiting people in their homes and it was not acceptable for me culturally to visit a home several times for follow-up on my own, especially to talk to women and girls.

Five years later, and my search for a wife ongoing, someone came to Egypt from Jordan to join the organization. It was part of my job to read all the application forms from people applying to join our teams, and as I was looking for a wife I was doubly interested to see if there was a girl who might be suitable! One day my attention was drawn to one particular application form. This person was a lady, thirty-three years old – the same age as me. I took an immediate interest in her as she had been offered a job and was already coming, and I felt that she was somebody I wanted to get to know in person!

While Magdy had been sharing his story, Rima, who was sat next to him on the sofa, had waited patiently to share hers. When Magdy handed her the microphone in order for her to share the story of their unusual courtship, Rima delightedly seized the opportunity and Magdy sat back to listen to his wife, all the while smiling broadly!

I had heard about the Lord many times from my brother and sister, but when the man I had loved so deeply took himself out of my life, I picked up a Bible and started to read the story of Paul and how Jesus changed the course of his life in one day. I knelt down and said, "Lord, for years I have been planning my life, but from now on I want to live your plan for my life, and I accept you as my Lord and Saviour."

It was a hard time experiencing the ending of a long relationship that had lasted seventeen years. But the day I accepted the Lord, I immediately felt a change in my life, and over the next two and a half years I felt drawn into full-time ministry. It was a strange calling for me and I didn't understand how it would work out. I left my job with an airline and heard the Lord calling me to go to Egypt. But I did not want to go to Egypt! I contacted a mission organization to see what opportunities they could offer me, thinking I would stay in Jordan, but to my horror and surprise they invited me to go and live in Egypt for one year, along with two other Jordanians.

At that time the whole Arab world had been turned upside down when Saddam Hussein's forces invaded Kuwait in August 1990,[45] and Jordan stood by Iraq and Egypt stood by Kuwait. There was a lot of trouble in Jordan during that August – the month I was planning to leave and go to Egypt. Regarding the two Jordanians who were due to travel to Egypt with me, the girl lost her passport and was unable to travel, and the boy travelled with me to Egypt, but at the airport they returned him to Jordan. So I found myself in Egypt alone, and my family were very concerned for me.

The first two weeks in Egypt were devastating for me. The culture and the way people lived were so different to what I was used to.

Magdy was leading the first training programme. During that first month, while I was coming to terms with the culture shock, the Lord was speaking to me through words in the Bible telling me to leave my country and leave my people. It seemed as though all the verses I was reading involved a leaving process.

I was certainly not thinking about marriage! After all, I had just experienced the breakdown of a relationship. I was thirty-three years old and had resigned myself to thinking that having reached that age, I would never get married; in our culture I was considered too old! I was giving my whole heart to serving the Lord, learning how to share the gospel and how to disciple new believers. I worked really hard but always at the back of my mind was the question, "When can I go back to Jordan?" I was a single girl, and in our culture it was unacceptable to step outside of the social and cultural norms.

Then the Lord starting speaking to me: "Two are better than one."

If I was in inner turmoil, the turmoil all around me was very real. As a Jordanian in Egypt at that time, there were days when it was too dangerous for me to go out because of the political tension spilling out onto the streets.

On New Year's Eve 1990, I was asking the Lord to forgive me for holding myself and my future from him. Another man had recently showed great interest in me although he did not propose to me. After giving consideration to whether or not I would like to marry him, I had rejected the thought. Having given up all hope of marriage, I decided I did not want to get married after all! But that night I put my life in the Lord's hands and again told Him my future was His.

Seven days later, the group of people I was training with were invited out for dinner at a friend's house. That night, as we were walking back home after the dinner, Magdy was walking next to me and he said, "Will you pray for me that in this coming year I achieve the goal the Lord is putting before me?"

I went home and prayed for Magdy. In my mind I saw two photographs, one of the man who had recently showed an interest in me, and the other of Magdy. "Choose," the Lord said. The feelings were getting stronger and stronger. Which one would I choose? I prayed to know whether the Lord was speaking to me or whether I was imagining all this. "Choose," the Lord said again.

"But Lord, I have just said no to the thought of getting married to this man. As for Magdy, I don't know anything about him except that he serves You only! He is seven years younger than me – I heard it from the girls – and I cannot marry a man who is seven years younger than me!"

Then I told the Lord that if I had to choose, I would choose Magdy for one reason: he was in the same ministry that I wanted to work in. I also asked the Lord that if He really was speaking to me, to show me Magdy's real age.

A few days later, Magdy's sister invited our group (which included Indians, Egyptians, and Jordanians) for dinner. As we were sat around the table, one of the girls asked Magdy his age! He answered, "I was born in 1957." I was shocked because I too was born in 1957! At that moment I felt the Lord was speaking directly to me and answering my prayer. I realized this was for real and I had to take the prospect of marriage to Magdy seriously.

I started to feel love towards Magdy but I had no idea what he felt about me. For two months my love towards Magdy grew, but at the same time I became tired of being in love again! I still did not know whether he had any feelings towards me. I was reading in Genesis where it said, "On the twenty-second of the second month the land dried." I said, "OK, Lord, on the twenty-second of February, if Magdy doesn't speak to me I will stop loving him and give up all hopes of marriage. Even if he comes on the twenty-third I will not respond!"

My birthday was on the third of February and my mum wanted to send me a bouquet of flowers, so she called my friend to ask her to organize this for her. This friend went to Magdy and said, "Rima's mum wants to send her a bouquet of flowers."

His response was, "Leave that to me!"

During this time, although I hadn't realized it, he had been developing a love towards me but didn't know what to do! So on my birthday he sent his friend to my house with a bouquet of flowers and asked me to sign a paper, which I thought was rather strange. There was a card with the flowers and I recognized the handwriting as Magdy's.

Later that afternoon one of the group leaders called me and asked me to confirm my signature on the piece of paper that I had signed earlier. "Is this your signature?" he asked.

"Yes," I replied.

"Why don't you take care what you sign?" he said.

"But this is only the paper from the flower shop. What's wrong?" I replied.

When he unfolded the paper I discovered that what I had signed, on the edge of the paper, was actually a fictitious marriage contract. I was very embarrassed and went away and cried. I didn't know what to do. Magdy had never spoken to me about marriage!

But that night, on my birthday, Magdy proposed to me. We both knew the Lord had brought us together, but I was concerned about what his family would think about me being a Jordanian and what my family would feel about me marrying an Egyptian. I told the Lord I would not agree to marry Magdy until after I had met his family.

The day we were due to meet his family, the Lord spoke to my heart that He was giving me a gift and I was not to put any conditions on whether or not to accept His gift. Later on I learned from Magdy that the Lord had spoken to him and that I was a gift to him. Magdy had, until then, been attracted to me partly because I had a new car! He admitted that he had wavered about starting a relationship with me, but after a time of prayer the Lord spoke to his heart that a gift from Him was vastly superior to a new car! It seemed that both of us had a different point of view about marriage that the Lord graciously changed.

My family were initially against our marriage and it was very hard. But then one of my sisters came to meet Magdy and his family because my family wanted to know all about them from somebody whose opinion they could trust. Jordanian social standards and protocol are very strict!

We finally got engaged in Jordan and Magdy's family came from Egypt for this occasion, which was a huge challenge for his mother because of the trouble between our two countries. But his family came and met my family and they both fell in love with each other!

However, we had to wait a further two months before we could get married because the mission organization we both worked for would not allow us to marry until we had been engaged for six months because we were from different cultures. This was very hard for both of us but during that time the Lord helped us to see something that was very shocking. We both had a blood test and the results showed that I was a diabetic. Until this time, I had no idea that I had diabetes. How could I marry Magdy now? I decided to break off our engagement and give him back the ring. I told him I had watched my father suffer from diabetes and I didn't want him to have to live with someone who might have to face the same fate. But Magdy would not accept this and instead said that we should pray and ask the Lord to show us His will.

Then Magdy came to me and said that the Lord had given me two "gifts", Magdy and diabetes, and I had to accept them both together! He was very gracious.

Six months after we were married I found out I was pregnant. As the time drew near for the baby to be born, two days before delivery, the baby girl died in my womb because of the diabetes. This was a big shock; we never expected such a thing to happen. We had hidden the issue of diabetes from everyone; we had kept it as "our little secret". But when the baby died people were asking why. It was very hard for us to lose our baby girl in this way and then to face explaining to the people around us why this had happened – sometimes not telling the whole truth. It was not like us – we both like to live in integrity with the Lord.

Eventually, two years later, I was pregnant again. But those two years of trying for another baby were a challenge because I was getting older; by this time I was thirty-five years old. Magdy tried to comfort me by saying, "Isn't it enough that we have an intimate relationship?" But this hurt me because I felt Magdy did not understand the pain I was going through and my deep desire to be a mother. In time he came to realize the true depth of my feelings.

In the meantime we had received biblical counselling that helped us to recover from the death of our daughter and had come to realize that hiding our little secret was not what the Lord would have us do; rather, He wanted us to share it. When we realized that the Lord was in control of our lives and it was a sin to not tell the whole truth to the people close to us, we confessed and told everybody that I had diabetes and this had been the reason for our daughter's death. As a result, the Lord brought peace into our lives and people prayed for us, and it wasn't long before I was pregnant again. Our son was born twenty years ago.

We moved to Israel from Egypt when he was very young so he has grown up here.

When we first came to Jerusalem, we pastored the Alliance Church in the Old City of Jerusalem. After that we moved to the Gaza Strip and worked with the pastor of the Baptist church there for four years, during which time there was much unrest. It was very challenging.

After that, we moved to Nazareth where we lived for two years. When Magdy became the director of a mission organization we moved back to Jerusalem as it is a strategic place from which to direct our ministry and meet with our staff working in different towns and cities in the land. Magdy then became the pastor of another Alliance church outside the Old City of Jerusalem.

Magdy takes up the story ...

When I started in the ministry and realized God was moving me from Alexandria to Cairo and then to the whole of Egypt and beyond to the Middle East during that time at the beginning of the 1990s, God gave me a burden and a love for the Muslims. This was a big challenge, because if I love Muslims then I have to share the gospel with them, and this was very risky in Egypt. At first, I found it difficult to accept this challenge and I delayed starting work in this area. But eventually, after the Lord reassured me, I began to have a vision for this work.

After working among Muslims in Egypt, by 1997 we were ready to serve the Lord outside the country. The opportunity presented itself when we received an invitation from the then leader of the Alliance Church in Jerusalem to come and work in Jerusalem among Muslims. Although at that time I had no experience of being the pastor of a church, we agreed to come and be the pastors and at the same time lead the church in how it could reach out to the local Muslim population in Jerusalem.

After two years of being a pastor in Jerusalem, God opened the door for us to move to Gaza. I was so happy about this opportunity because in Gaza there were only a few Christians! I would be swimming in an ocean of Muslims! I went to assist the pastor of the Baptist church there, and for us it was the best opportunity we had ever had to see people becoming believers in Jesus and to be able to disciple so many people.

After four years in Gaza, I felt it was time to focus on providing Muslim-background believers in Jesus (MBBs) with their own churches or fellowship groups meeting in homes. Today we have a home church here in Jerusalem for believers in Jesus from Muslim backgrounds. We are spending a lot of our time working among both the men and the women, discipling them in their faith, teaching them how to be good husbands and parents, leading them, and encouraging them to have a better relationship with God and with each other. From our experience in caring, leading, and pastoring different churches, home groups, and families from different backgrounds, we see the most important challenge is how to build godly, healthy, and strong relationships in order to have a healthy family life and church life. If they can lead their family then they can start to be leaders in the church.

When I look at what God is doing here in Israel, I stand amazed at the numbers of believers in Jesus coming from different backgrounds. If this trend continues, we will see many new churches springing up in Israel and the wider Middle East in the coming months and years, and we pray that they will have the agape love among them to affect the next generation.

CHAPTER 7

Sandy Shoshani – the Cost of Believing in Yeshua

There are various prophecies in the Bible that describe the Jewish diaspora,[46] including these verses from the prophet Hosea:

> For the Israelites will live for many days without king or prince, without sacrifice or sacred stones, without ephod or idol. Afterwards the Israelites will return and seek the Lord their God and David their king. They will come trembling to the Lord and to his blessings in the last days.[47]

Jesus also predicted the destruction of Jerusalem that later happened in AD 70, resulting in the Jewish people fleeing Israel and eventually dispersing around the world:

> As he approached Jerusalem and saw the city, he wept over it and said, "If you, even you, had only known on this day what would bring you peace – but now it is hidden from your

**eyes. The days will come upon you when your
enemies will build an embankment against
you and encircle you and hem you in on every
side. They will dash you to the ground, you and
the children within your walls. They will not
leave one stone on another, because you did not
recognise the time of God's coming to you."[48]**

Other prophecies predict the return of Jewish people from around the world to live in Israel, such as this prophecy from Ezekiel:

**"I will bring you from the nations and gather
you from the countries where you have been
scattered."[49]**

In seeking to understand what God is doing in Israel in these days, it is helpful to recall these prophecies and appreciate their fulfilment. Perhaps what is most thought provoking is that biblical prophecy is being fulfilled in the days in which we live as more and more Jewish people move from the nations to which they dispersed all those years ago, back to their homeland of Israel.

Sandy Shoshani's story is another story providing evidence of this fulfilment. Today she is the National Director of Be'ad Chaim, the Israel Pro Life organization, and lives with her husband and their seven children in Maale Adumim, east of Jerusalem. She was brought up in a traditional Jewish family in the United States of America. Her parents were pious Jews and desirous to raise their daughter so that she would maintain Jewish tradition and faith.

I met Sandy at her office in Jerusalem where she shared her story. It is a story that demonstrates the cost that so many Jewish people are prepared to pay when they come to realize that Yeshua is the Messiah. For Sandy, this also involved leaving America and coming to Israel – a journey that her father insisted she make. As you will read, Sandy came reluctantly at first.

I had a lovely childhood. I was raised by loving parents. We went to the synagogue every Shabbat. I knew all the prayers by heart. I went to public school and also Hebrew school where I learned to speak Hebrew fluently, although I never intended to come and live in Israel. My parents raised money for Israel; my father thought that raising money was enough!

My parents had great ambitions for me. My mother, who was a religious Jew, wanted me to be a religious Jew. They were later to be very disappointed when I came to believe in Yeshua, the Messiah.

All my life I was seeking God. However, even though I knew the prayers by heart and we observed all the Jewish holidays, I always felt a certain distance from God. As a small child I remember calling up to Him and saying, "Where are you God? If you are real, I want to know you."

It was during my last few years at high school that I began to become extremely interested in ideas from different religions, and in my last year at school I was into Buddha, Krishna, and Bahai. I was looking for the living God. I knew Judaism was a beautiful, rich religion, but I wanted to know the living God.

Many Israelis, after serving their time in the army, go abroad – often to India or South America. Why? Because they are looking, seeking for God.

When I went to university in Chicago, during the first week there my Catholic roommate (I had never met her until we were thrown together at university) came in and said, "I have just become a Christian."

I said, "You are a Christian – you're Catholic."

She said, "No, you don't understand. I've given my life to God now. I've been born again."

Well, I didn't understand and she made me very angry because she would read her Bible and pray every morning. So to counter this, I would stand in the middle of the room with my Jewish Siddur (prayer book) and pray. Gradually I became more religious and started going to the Jewish University Organization.

For three months I was nasty to her and asked her questions in anger, not out of genuine interest. She would calmly answer, "I don't know the answers to all your questions, but I do know that Christ died for you and He rose from the dead. I don't know anything else." It made me so angry. I was the Jew. I was the one who had God!

Then one day I was out walking and I felt compelled in my heart to consider my life. Now I know that was the Holy Spirit, but I didn't understand that then. I felt that my life was like a weighing scale, the sort you find in the marketplace. On the one hand everything was good. I had perfect grades. I had a boyfriend. I had loving parents. I had plenty of money. What more could an eighteen-year-old want? But on the other hand I had no satisfaction. I didn't know why I was alive.

As I made my way back to the dormitory that day, I passed somebody who was making a lot of noise. I screamed at her, "Shut up, you're bothering everybody!"

She replied, "Do you know what, try to change yourself."

Those words were like a knife in my heart, and I can't explain this except to say that I know God moves in our hearts when He wants to reveal Himself. I began to feel the weight of my judgment and criticism; the evil in my heart. We don't usually think about these things when we're only eighteen, but on that day these things were weighing on my mind. I found myself weeping and weeping and weeping. I wept all night. My roommate didn't know what to do or say so she called the man who had shared the gospel with her.

A young woman, who was a Jewish believer, came and showed me Isaiah 53. She showed me from this chapter that someone had died to carry the weight of our sins. He died like a lamb led to the slaughter without saying a word. I didn't know who this person was until the man came a few hours later and read to me verses from Matthew and John and asked, "Who is this who died?"

I said, "I don't know, but I read about him in Isaiah also." The two merged for me.

He said, "Can you believe this?"

I said, "I don't know anything."

He said, "Would you be willing to take a jump of faith and say 'Jesus, Yeshua, if you are real, reveal yourself. I want you.' If he's not real, nothing will happen, so what will you have lost?"

And so I did that. I felt as though I was jumping off a cliff into deep water. I prayed, "If you are real, I want you." I've never looked back. He showed Himself to me in my heart and He became my dearest friend.

When I went home to Boston immediately before the Christmas break I prayed, "I won't tell them I'm a believer in Yeshua unless they ask me directly."

We were sitting at dinner one night and my dad said, "How can anybody believe that the Messiah can come from a virgin? How can anybody believe anything so stupid, that a virgin would give birth and that God would come from a person?"

I looked at him and said, "Well, maybe there is something in it."

My mother, who was sitting across the table from me, looked directly into my eyes and said, "Do you believe in Jesus?"

So I said, "Yes."

But they thought it was another one of my "things", and during that year my parents left me alone for about three months. But when I returned home for the spring break they started sending me to rabbis. They talked with me, verbally fought with me. A rabbi was a brilliant man with a PhD, I couldn't answer his questions or reply to his comments. But I knew one thing – that Yeshua lived in my heart and I could not deny His reality. I could not deny the reality of my experience with the living God who I had sought for so long.

During the next three years, while I was an undergraduate, my parents would argue with me, but not in a horrible way. However, during my fourth year of studies, my mother became ill with cancer and they blamed me for her cancer: my father, my mother, the rabbi, the family. They asked me to give up my faith in order to save my mother's life. But I couldn't give up my faith. That would have been impossible. You can't believe something and then say, "I don't believe."

Then they made me promise that I would marry a Jew. I promised my mother, when she was dying, that I would marry a Jewish man and I promised that I would stop living with Christian roommates. In the last conversation I had with my mother she asked me why I had to give my life to this new faith; why couldn't I just live a "normal" life?

I said, "If you believe in something with all your heart, you have to serve with all your heart; you can't be half-hearted." I reminded her that she was the one who had given me a passion for God. "You gave me a passion for God, and now I know Him and I love Him."

When she passed away, of course we were all deeply sad and hurt and grieving. My father, in his sorrow, blamed me. During the year following my mother's death, he would phone and say very harsh things to me and I would reply, "Dad, thank you for sharing your heart with me. I love you." Then I would cry out to God for His help and His healing.

At the end of the year, when I had finished my master's degree programme, my father told me that he wanted me to go to a special programme for intensive Jewish studies. The rabbis were reluctant to take me into the programme, so required an interview prior to accepting me. During the course of the interview, I realized that the programme would be very difficult for me emotionally and that I would perhaps suffer a nervous breakdown as a result. My father was determined that I enter this programme. The Lord had told me to do whatever my father said; I wasn't to deny Him, but I was to obey my father in love. So I agreed. The teachers (rabbis) persuaded me, through a form of brainwashing, that I had killed my mother and that if I continued to believe, I would kill my father. I felt terribly guilty and afraid.

Up until that time, my whole life had been spent in America. I had many good friends who were believers and I was about to start training for mission work. The rabbis encouraged me to make a fresh start and to leave my Christian friends and relationships. They encouraged me that I should leave America, leave everybody I knew, and go and live in Israel.

The rabbi arranged for me to go and study in a yeshiva, a Jewish place of study. I agreed to go. But then they also insisted that I publicly deny the Lord. And this I am most ashamed of: I did stand up and say I deny the Lord because I was so broken and was convinced I had killed my mother. I am deeply ashamed about that, but God has ministered to me about that through the life of Peter: three times he denied the Lord before coming back and serving the Lord – he was even crucified upside down for serving the Lord. I know that God is merciful and forgiving, but it was a very hard time.

Just before I left America to fly to Israel, I met with my former roommate, the previously Catholic girl who had come to faith, to say goodbye. She asked me if I would take the names of three believers in Israel. She is a very special person. She doesn't have a lot to say; she just cares. She said, "Go, pray, and do something with yourself. I have nothing to say to you, you are so confused. You don't know how to believe. Your heart is broken. "

My heart was broken. I had promised my father and the rabbi that I wouldn't pray in Yeshua's name again. I was carrying the guilt of my mother's death. I had denied my faith in Yeshua. I went for a walk and asked God to either take my life or reveal Himself in such a strong way that I would know what to do.

I got on the plane from Boston to Tel Aviv. I had a layover in London. While waiting in Heathrow airport I heard the Lord say to me, "Open Psalm 40."

But I said, "No, Lord, the Bible doesn't speak to me any more. I can't."

He said, "Just read the psalm."

And the psalm said:

> He lifted me out of the slimy pit,
> out of the mud and mire;
> he set my feet on a rock
> and gave me a firm place to stand.
> He put a new song in my mouth,
> a hymn of praise to our God.
> Many will see and fear the Lord
> and put their trust in him.

And He gave me a new song, and I felt God spoke to me in my ears and said, "Jesus is Lord, don't be afraid." I felt oil pouring from my head all the way down to my feet, and I knew that Yeshua was the Lord.

I had experienced the power of God in the airport on my way to Israel, I had experienced His voice reassuring me that Yeshua is Lord, and I landed in Israel not knowing anybody. I took a cab to the yeshiva, and when I spoke to the rabbi there he said, "I understand that you were a believer in Yeshua but that you are not any more."

I said, "No, I am. But for the sake of my father I am willing to study here."

And the rabbi rejected me. He said, "I don't want you here because I am afraid that your questions will confuse the other students."

It was 1979. I was in Israel with no place to go. I didn't know anybody. I didn't know what to do. The rabbi told me that I could sleep in the infirmary of the yeshiva for three days until I could find myself an apartment.

So I decided to walk to the Wailing Wall. On my way I saw a shop with Bibles in the window. I thought it was a Jewish Bible shop. I felt persuaded to go into the shop and ask the man about his religion. I felt so awkward that I walked up to the door and away again three times!

Finally I opened the door and walked up to the man behind the counter and said, "Sir, I'm so embarrassed to ask you this but could you please tell me your religion."

He looked at the floor and he said, "I am a Jew who believes in the Messiah Yeshua."

I was amazed! I said, "I have the names of three believers in Israel. Could you please help me?"

The first name was a woman. "I am sorry, she lives in Tel Aviv. I can't help you."

The next name: "I'm sorry, he's too busy to talk to you."

The third name was of a Baptist pastor in Jerusalem called Bob Lindsay. "Could you tell me how to find this man?"

The man in the bookshop said, "Turn round, he's opening the door!" and Bob Lindsay walked into the shop.

"Sir, could you help me?" I asked him, "I've just come through brainwashing and have had a terrible time."

He said, "Come tomorrow morning." He prayed with me for healing and deliverance and said, "Come to the congregation on Saturday."

On Saturday I went to what was then called The Baptist House. There were only two Messianic congregations in Jerusalem at that time and only a few hundred believers in the whole of Israel. I met some other believers there and within one week I had an apartment with a believer in Jerusalem, and I had a part-time job (I was also studying Hebrew at a higher level).

I didn't intend staying for long; I was planning to stay for one year and then return home to America, but in order to work I had to have a work permit. So I went to the Ministry of the Interior and said to them, "Could I please have a work permit."

She said, "What is your name?" My maiden name was Levin. She then asked, "And what is your mother's maiden name."

"Shapiro," I replied.

She said, "I'm sorry, but you are making aliyah!"

I said, "But I don't want to make aliyah."

She said, "You must, you are Jewish." She put a stamp on my passport and within two weeks I was an Israeli citizen. God directed my life. He wanted me here. He led me as a loving Father.

I got a job in my profession as a speech therapist even though my Hebrew was not yet good enough to be a speech therapist. God just kept me here.

My dad remarried. I wanted to go back to America but my boss reminded me that I had a contract and I could take a vacation, but I must return to my work at the hospital.

The next year I met my Israeli husband. The very first time I met him was in the apartment of one of my friends in Jerusalem. He didn't know Yeshua at that time. He was in his soldier's uniform and later, on the way home, we rode together on the bus. "Well, it's been good to meet you," he said, not thinking we would ever meet again.

The next time I saw him was when I came with an unbelieving friend to meet his sister, who was a believer. He was there and joined in our conversation, and a few weeks later he came to faith. The person who brought him to faith brought him to meet me. We didn't realize it at the time, but she was matchmaking!

The reason it took him so long to come to faith was because he was weighing up the cost of such a decision. Was he prepared to give his life? When he came to faith, all he did was eat the Word of God. He read the Bible for hours each day. He wept. He repented. He became a strong believer.

We were engaged within three months and we were married six months later. During our first five years of marriage, my husband studied in Haifa and received his engineering degree. He later worked in his profession for thirteen years in the Jerusalem area. During all of these years he was very active in the congregation and served as an elder. In 2004, the Lord spoke to him and told him to leave his profession and become a full-time pastor. He said, "We have seven children. I'll leave if you give me an income."

Well, that wasn't the Lord's plan. He said, "You leave." And so a year later my husband left his well-paid profession and became a full-time pastor (with a symbolic, very minimal salary).

My husband is a very solid, serious, humble person and the Lord told him, "Don't despise small beginnings." Our congregation was at first a house group that came out of the King of Kings English-speaking congregation that meets in Jerusalem. It has grown now to more than two hundred people. Two-thirds of our congregation are under twenty-five years old – babies, children, students, soldiers, young adults.

How did I feel about my husband giving up a well-paid job to take on a voluntary position? During the first year of our marriage the Lord told me to trust my husband with our finances and major decisions as they were his responsibility under God. I have never looked back on that decision and I have never worried about our finances. So when he told me the Lord had told him to step out in faith, he was the concerned one, not me. However, him being a pastor was another story because I did not want to be a pastor's wife! I was concerned about the weight and the burden of it. I had been teaching at a pre-school and the Lord told me to stop teaching. I had no problem with that and was prepared to be a full-time pastor's wife. I didn't seek to be a pastor's wife, but if that was what God wanted me to do, I was happy with that.

However, a year after the Lord told me to stop teaching, I was invited by the board of Be'ad Chaim, Israel Pro Life, to become the director. I told them I was not interested. They asked me if I would be willing to talk to the board. I agreed and again they asked me if I would be interested in becoming the director. Again, I declined. As far as I was concerned, Israel had many problems within its society: why would I want to commit my life to this work? They asked me to take some books and videos about abortion and return in a month to talk further.

By the end of the month, I had learned the hard realities of abortion in Israel. I was challenged and compelled to take action by some verses in the book of Proverbs:

If you falter in a time of trouble,
how small is your strength!
Rescue those being led away to death;
hold back those staggering toward slaughter.
If you say, "But we knew nothing about this,"
does not he who weighs the heart perceive it?
Does not he who guards your life know it?
Will he not repay each person according to what he
has done?[50]

Be'ad Chaim is a national organization with twelve centres across Israel. We encourage mothers to keep their baby rather than have an abortion. We help them in every possible way to keep their baby. We finance the baby for one year through an initiative called Operation Moses; we provide all the baby needs, including a cot and bedding, a pushchair, a bath, nappies, clothing, and food. Most of our centres have a counsellor and a baby boutique with clothes and items for the baby.

Be'ad Chaim was started in the early 1980s by a group of dedicated Christian believers, together with local believers, who were concerned about the high abortion rate in Israel at that time. Even now, approximately every fifth pregnancy is terminated in abortion in Israel. The government funds the abortions for the women through national health insurance. During those early years, several babies were saved annually because only counselling and emotional support were available, but after beginning the Operation Moses project in 2006, the numbers of babies saved grew dramatically.

Most of the Israeli women who consider abortion are poor. Out of nearly eight million people living in Israel today, 1.8 million are living below the poverty line. A hundred thousand children are living in poverty.

When I started working here in 2005 I was invited to speak to a congregation in Tel Aviv about the work. Afterwards the pastor came to me and said, "It's not enough just to pray. What can we do?"

I said, "I don't know. What do you want to do?"

They began the Operation Moses project to supply everything a mother would need for the first year of the baby's life. They funded the programme for one year, but then the pastor had to leave the country and we had to take over funding the programme. In the first year, fifteen babies were saved; the year after the number rose to forty. But then it started to grow, and as it grew, so the costs increased! Each baby was costing 1,200 euros.

Six months after Be'ad Chaim took over the running of the programme, our funds were depleted and my board came to me and told me to stop the programme. I said no: "This is God's programme. He started this; He will be faithful." We had fifty pregnant women on our list at that time and we were committed to meeting their needs. It was amazing to watch how God supplied all those needs. As each baby was born so we would have enough money to support it. The more money we received, the more babies we saved, and the more babies we saved, the more money would come in. It was amazing. From 2006 to 2014 we were able to save more than 800 babies. At the present time we are supporting 350 women; just over 100 are pregnant and the remainder are mothers with babies under one year old.

Sometimes we hear about women through social workers, but many find us on Google and come to us through our website; others come through word of mouth. We have a hotline number so when somebody calls, one of our counsellors will answer and encourage the person to come and meet with a counsellor in the centre closest to them.

Once we can get the person to come and sit with us, we can save more than 95 per cent of the babies. Our counsellors are trained to listen and love and give hope. We are not telling her, "Don't have an abortion." Rather we are telling her, "The best thing for you and your life is to keep that child and we're going to help you."

I see it like an onion: the core is that the mother loves the baby and wants to keep the child, but the problems, the onion layers, cover that natural instinct to love and she feels overwhelmed and has no option. They often to say to us, "Pro-choice? I have no choice." But we give her choice. We enable her to keep the child by providing for her and befriending her and giving her physical and emotional support, and spiritual support too if we are able to pray for her and encourage her to draw closer to God.

Recently, because of their difficult situations, we have been able to help many women who have come to Israel from Ethiopia. However, the vast majority of the women we have helped are Israeli-born Jews from broken families, single mothers whose mothers were also single mothers; some are young girls still at school. But it is not true to think that most women wanting an abortion are young; 45 per cent of women having an abortion are married. Many couples are living on or below the poverty line, and if they have another child, this reduces their chance of ever lifting themselves out of the poverty trap. With poverty being such a major issue, once they hear that we can support them, this is what makes the difference between life and death. In Israel, within one year a mother should be able to place her child in daycare and get a job.

Our counsellors are women who care about other people. Many of them have had abortions and understand the conflict of an unplanned pregnancy and the pain of abortion. A large percentage of our counsellors are from Russian or Ukrainian backgrounds and understand the mindset of women from Russia where abortion is used as a form of birth control. We have met and ministered to women who have had as many as thirteen abortions. Women who have suffered the consequences of abortion often become passionate defenders of life.

My best counsellors are not those who have studied abortion. My best counsellors are those who seek the Lord and spend lots of time in prayer. They love their clients. And when our clients are loved, they know it.

Talking to Sandy Shoshani it was clear that at Be'ad Chaim, they care about the mothers who turn to them for help as much as they care about their babies. As Sandy said,

It is not uncommon for us to ask God to bless the child in the womb, bless the mother, provide work, bring health – bless, bless, bless! Their hearts are touched by our love and compassion for them. Our desire is chaim (life) both for mother and child. We want to bring new HOPE into their lives.

Sandy's own experience of the pain and heartbreak caused by her experience of rejection by close family members and her subsequent healing through her love of and faith in Yeshua has undoubtedly enabled her to use her life story to help others and quite literally save lives. She exudes enthusiasm for her work with Be'ad Chaim; it's far more than just a job for her. She is always on the lookout for ways to relieve the suffering of those who come to her. Some mothers require extra help, as she told me …

In 2014, we opened the House of Life where we can care for three mothers who need special help for coping with life with a young baby. Mothers are offered training in a wide variety of skills, including financial planning, cooking, and basic childcare, and also receive counselling.

As well as encouraging mothers to keep their babies, Sandy Shoshani recognizes the pain of those who have lost children through abortion.

In 2010, the Gardens of Life was dedicated as a place where women and men from all over the world are welcome to come and plant a tree in memory of a baby who was never born. These gardens offer healing because if somebody has had an abortion or a miscarriage, they often feel that they have never done anything for that child. This is an opportunity to plant a tree in memory of the child and to do something to get freedom and closure. We are developing this garden to provide a life path, a path people can walk through and take steps of healing and forgiveness and receive God's mercy and freedom for the loss after that abortion.

Looking to the future, I believe God will enable us to save many more babies and support the mothers so that they know they are not alone.

CHAPTER 8

Nashat Filmon – a Christian Arab in the Old City of Jerusalem

In 2008, Nashat Filmon became director of the Palestinian Bible Society based in Jerusalem. Although his work involves him working mainly with Palestinian people, Nashat also works in close cooperation with the Messianic and Arab Israeli team of the Bible Society in Israel; they share a common goal which is to make the Bible available to all.

Nashat's own story is complex and, like so many people you read about in this book, his life has been shaped by the challenge of growing up in Jerusalem and living with danger, conflict, and hostility. But, as you are about to read, it is these difficulties that have honed Nashat and developed his faith, enabling him to do the sensitive and often dangerous work he is now involved in.

I first met Nashat in Jerusalem one morning in February 2012. When I walked into his office he was engrossed in watching an Arabic news channel on television. Although the reporter was speaking in Arabic, the pictures told the story – the centre of Cairo had been brought to a standstill by thousands of protestors. The Arab "spring" had spilled onto the streets of the city, people were being killed, and tension was in the air.

Nashat has a personal interest in Egypt because his father is Egyptian. He began to tell me the story of how and why he came to be living in Jerusalem, a story that has in turn been shaped by world events.

My father came to Jerusalem in 1965, two years before the Six-Day War in 1967.[51] He was sent to work in Jerusalem by an Egyptian para-church organization that supported Christian ministry in the Middle East and the repair and upkeep of biblical sites in the region. He came to Jerusalem, initially for two years, to help with some reconstruction work that was taking place at the Coptic convent and Church of the Holy Sepulchre[52] in the Old City (also known as the Church of the Resurrection). After that work was completed he decided to stay for a little longer, but the war erupted and he was unable to return to Egypt. However, during that time he met my mother. She was born and grew up in Jerusalem and her father was the pastor of a church in the Old City. My father used to go to this church from time to time, which is where he met my mother. After they were married they made their home in Jerusalem, so this is how I came to be here!

I have many memories of growing up in the Old City of Jerusalem. There is something significant about living here because there are so many biblical sites.

From the roof of my parents' home I could see the Church of the Holy Sepulchre, the Mount of Olives, and the Temple Mount where the golden Dome of the Rock and the Al Aqsa Mosque stand today. All around us were churches and holy sites. While it is a special place, it is also a challenging place to live. It is not possible to drive a car through the narrow streets so we walked a great deal!

I grew up during two intifadas,[53] and that was difficult because for many years we were not allowed to leave our immediate neighbourhood. We would go to school in the morning and then come home. We were not allowed to go far because many things could happen to us: we could be arrested, or beaten up, or even shot. Many of the people we knew who lived around us were attacked in this way.

But in hindsight, I look back on those early years of my life as being a good experience, and although I no longer live in the Old City, when I return to visit people there it always feels very special to belong to this place. Sometimes, because you see all these sights every day, you miss out on the significance of the places and what they represent. Living so close to the Church of the Holy Sepulchre, which in Arabic is called the Church of the Resurrection (which I prefer as a name), is very special because that is where Jesus died and came back to life again.

Growing up during troubled times meant that I experienced a "them and us" situation which was an ongoing challenge. My father, who was a straightforward, humble man who used to drive a truck, was one of the very few people who spoke Hebrew in our neighbourhood. As a child I only spoke Arabic, but outside the Old City, just a few minutes' walk from our house, the people there spoke only Hebrew. Language was perhaps one of the biggest barriers or challenges between "us and them". Not being able to understand or be understood made communication between us impossible.

Also, our culture was totally different to the Jewish culture. Being a Palestinian Christian living in the Old City among and part of the bigger Muslim culture, the local mindset of the Muslims towards Jewish people became our mindset, which I now know to be wrong. For example, we would refer to "the Jews" as a collective term even though they came from many different backgrounds. In just the same way, "the Jews" called us "the Arabs", even though we came from many different backgrounds and denominations – Armenian, Greek Orthodox, or Coptic Christians. From my perspective as a child, growing into a young man, the things that divided us seemed insurmountable and could have had an adverse effect on my attitude towards Israel and the Jewish people.

There were so many restrictions placed on us, so many places we could not visit. These feelings of being hemmed in and confined to a small, clearly defined area were compounded when, through my father's work as a driver, I sometimes had the opportunity to go and visit "them". When I saw how "they" lived, I saw how we Palestinians were deprived of the basic things in life – the freedom to move, the freedom to do things when we liked – and I, along with my friends, always felt that we were considered inferior by the Israeli people. As a child, and later as a teenager, this affected my thinking and emotions. In addition, the Israeli army was always present in the Old City, next to our homes and our schools. The soldiers would stop us in the street and ask us where we lived and demand that we show them our identity cards. The problem was, this was our only encounter with Jewish people and therefore we did not develop a healthy or positive relationship with them. Inevitably, feelings of hatred and animosity developed in me and I felt envious of the freedom Jewish people had compared to us Palestinians, and I started asking why we had to tolerate so much suffering.

However, I must add that I grew up in a very healthy environment at home. My mum is a wonderful Christian lady: she cared for all human beings regardless of their background, and her influence on me was considerable and tempered my feelings of frustration.

My dream as a young man was to own a high-class restaurant or hotel where I could welcome people and sit and talk with them and ensure they were taken good care of. After leaving school I studied hotel and restaurant management at Bethlehem University for three years. During this time I also had a part-time job in a hotel, and when I completed my studies I was offered the job of manager of that hotel, which incorporated a high-class restaurant. At the same time

I received another job offer from the Bible Society. I had to choose between the two. What was I to do?

At that time the Lord was working in my heart. I submitted all my dreams and personal ambitions to Him. A defining moment in my life occurred when I was invited to a meeting in a church in the Old City of Jerusalem. I went, and the subject the speaker was talking about was the End Days. It was challenging for me: could I submit my hopes and dreams to Him and refuse such a good job opportunity? It had been my lifelong ambition to manage a hotel, and now the opportunity was there. However, that night, the Lord touched my heart and I decided, without hesitation, to join the Bible Society.

And so it was that in 1995 I became the manager of a Christian bookshop rather than the manager of a hotel! At that time the bookshop was based just outside the Old City. Just as I was beginning my work there I discovered something that really surprised me – my grandfather had worked for the Bible Society when he was a young man! Not only that, but an uncle, along with another relative, had also enjoyed close connections with the Bible Society! And so I realized there was something quite unique regarding the connection between the Bible Society and our family, and I was following in a family tradition!

So that's how my working life began. I was very young and the manager of a small bookshop where we gave away more Bibles than we sold! Welcoming people and helping them in their spiritual journey to discover the Bible became my focus. I felt that although the Lord had led me to study hotel and restaurant management, now He had brought me into a similar situation where I could use my training to serve spiritual food to people. I quickly came to appreciate that in many ways the training I had received was highly relevant in the Bible bookshop because whether I was serving customers with food to eat or with spiritual food, it had to be done with the right attitude: with respect, always with a smile, and in a way that honoured the person who was receiving it. From the first day that I started working with the Bible Society, I have always found it a great privilege to be involved in "serving" people with the Word of God.

In those early days I was still a single man and also very interested in the media. So after closing the bookshop every day, I would work late into the night producing radio programmes and short videos about the Bible and the Christian life that could be given to people coming into the bookshop. This was part of a new ministry that I co-founded, called JEO (Jerusalem Evangelistic Outreach). I was so happy to be doing this work that I didn't mind working such long hours!

The Bible Society also has a student centre in the university town of Bir Zeit,[54] in the West Bank, and another of my responsibilities was to coordinate the work there. It wasn't long before we needed to find somebody to help with the work there, so we advertised the job and many people applied. We drew up a shortlist of three people and I was on the interview panel.

On the day of the interview a beautiful girl came in wearing a red jacket. She sat down and we started asking her questions about her life and her career. I was immediately impressed by her and we employed her because she was the most suitable applicant for the job. However, I also felt that I had met somebody who would become special to me and felt that this was a relationship that I would like to develop when the time was right.

A couple of years later we started going out with each other and now she is my wife. She is a Palestinian. She was born in Jerusalem and grew up in Ramallah in the West Bank.

As things stand today, I am a Jerusalemite with Israeli ID which enables me to travel anywhere within Israel and the West Bank. My wife, however, because she grew up in the West Bank, has to apply annually for permission from the Israeli military to live as my wife with me in Jerusalem. She is not allowed to drive or work or travel from Ben Gurion airport. She is allowed only to be with us at home and so we live with a number of restrictions on our lives, which makes life very difficult at times.

In 2008 Nashat was made director of the Palestinian Bible Society for East Jerusalem, the West Bank, and Gaza. He is part of a team called Bible Lands that includes Victor Kalisher, a Messianic Jew and director of the Israeli Bible Society based in Jerusalem, and Diana Katanacho, who leads the work in the north of Israel among Arab Israelis. Remarkably, perhaps, they are united in a heartfelt shared concern for both people groups – Jews and Arabs/ Palestinians.

The Palestinian Bible Society team works among people living East Jerusalem, the West Bank, and the Gaza strip where 99 per cent of the population are Muslim. In the early 1990s we were simply giving away Bibles to people who asked for their own copy, but today we find that people have many other needs as well and so our work has had to address their physical hunger as well as their spiritual hunger. The Bible, especially the New Testament, carries little meaning to Muslim people because they widely believe it has been corrupted and is therefore irrelevant today. Therefore we had to change our approach.

Today, while we continue to provide the Word of God in a language the Palestinian people can understand, at the same time we have begun to develop some community care projects whereby we can help people with their physical needs. In Gaza we are currently helping 100 (Muslim) families every month with essential food and clothing. We are also running micro-enterprise projects to enable people to start their own business in order to earn a living and provide for their families. For example, the Gaza Strip is situated by the sea on the Mediterranean so we give people who can catch fish the nets they need so that they can catch and then sell fresh fish in the local markets. We have provided others who can drive with reliable cars so they can organize and run taxi services. We are also running courses throughout the West Bank including English classes, computer courses, cultural evenings, and activities for children and young people in order to instil hope and a sense of purpose into a population who generally believe they are living in a hopeless situation.

We have grown from a team of three to a team of more than thirty people and many volunteers. The Lord has really blessed our work and now we have at least twelve centres and more than twenty programmes throughout the West Bank and the Gaza Strip.

Recently a Muslim lady in the West Bank approached one of our workers and asked her why the Bible Society was so involved in helping her and others in the community. She said we were closer to her than many of her own family members. Our answer to her was simple: we love you and care for you just as you are. This lady then started to cry and said, "I've never seen such love in my life before." We were able then to spend some quality time talking to her and praying for her.

This is the work we believe the Lord wants us involved in today – to show the love of God to these people who are so hungry and desperate to be loved.

Looking at the wider Middle East and the recent turmoil in the Arab world, which started in Tunisia in 2010, the streets of Cairo and other Arab nations have since erupted into violence, and it seems as though everybody has been surprised at how quickly this revolution exploded.

In Egypt there are approximately 10 million Coptic Christians; the Christian Coptic Church[55] has been in Egypt for centuries. Coming from a Coptic Christian background myself, I care deeply for them and for the country of Egypt. I look at the recent troubles there and my heart is divided. On the one hand, finally there is a measure of freedom from dictatorship with some hope for a democratic future where people feel that their vote counts and there is the hope of a better future. But on the other hand, I look and see a very dark side to the current situation. More Islamic fundamentalists are taking over the reins of power. Those who were seeking freedom are now seemingly in the minority; they still have a voice but their voice is not strong enough to make significant changes on the ground.

This mixed situation makes me want to pray earnestly for the Arab world and pray for God's plan for them. I know that there are many wonderful believers throughout the Arab countries. They are true seekers. Many have seen visions and had dreams of Jesus, and they know that usually when Christians are persecuted the natural response is for the church to grow. We have witnessed this in various places, including Iran. The reason the church is so strong in Egypt is because it has suffered persecution for many years.

I pray that the gospel, the Word of God, will continue to spread in Egypt. I pray that we would witness a true reconciliation. I believe the heart of the Lord is about reconciliation, bringing people to a place of reconciliation with God which then makes it possible to reconcile people together.

When I look at what is happening in the Gaza Strip (which shares a border with Egypt), Syria, Tunisia, and

Libya, and watch as the Islamic fundamentalist groups are gaining power, I just wonder what is going to happen in the future and how the politics and ideology of the Middle East is going to shift and change. I pray that out of all of this the Lord's will be done, and I believe that His will is for both Arabs and Israelis to find salvation.

My heart and my vision is to see peace in the Middle East. I believe that when we have peace, we can reach the people living in these troubled areas with the gospel. On the one hand, the church always seems to need a push from the back – persecution – to keep it on track. On the other hand, if the church is to reach out to people, peace is required.

I believe that there is a spiritual dimension to everything that happens in the world. I have no doubt that the Lord is allowing certain things to happen in order that His purposes can come to fulfilment. At the same time, I believe that the church has to wake up and has to be an activist in God's plan and has to continue reaching out to those hungry, thirsty, and needy families throughout all the Arab countries.

I remember being in Egypt and seeing a church called Moqattam[56] which is situated in a garbage village in Cairo; it's a fantastic place. This church is built into a cave in the rock and accommodates 10 to15,000 people. It has not been easy for these people who have had to cut into the rock face to carve out a cave in which they can meet. To establish and build a church in the Middle East it has to be built on the Rock, and Jesus is our Rock and we have to stand close to Him. This is my call to all Christians in this region, that unless we stand on the Rock, we will collapse. Rock also represents the hardships that we have to go through, being in the Middle East where just being a Christian requires a calling. Most of the Christian friends I grew up with have left the country because of the conflict and the many wars. It's a calling to be here, to stay here, and to serve here.

Many Christians living in Egypt are concerned that some of their number will leave the country as life becomes harder for them and they lose their rights and their freedom. These are people who believe there is little hope for the future of the church there. Others, though, feel they want to stay: these are Christian people who are prepared to stay and fight for their rights and for a stronger voice in the Egyptian parliament. I understand those who want to leave for the sake of their children, and I also love those who want to stay and be salt and light in that difficult and dangerous situation in their nation; this again is a calling.

When I search the Scriptures to see what they have to say about the times in which we live, I find there are many passages, especially in the New Testament, that talk about salvation. For example, in John's Gospel we read, "For God so loved the whole world that He gave His one and only Son ..."[57] I believe this verse speaks very clearly into our situation today in that God intends for everybody to be saved and know Jesus Christ.

The story of Saul who became Paul when God turned his life around when he was riding along the road from Jerusalem to Damascus[58] is the story of many Arabs. Once they were enemies of the gospel and hated the gospel because they felt it was not right. But with a divine touch from the Lord, through a vision or a dream, God is turning this enemy into His friend; and not just a friend but an evangelist, an activist, somebody who works for the gospel and is totally devoted to the work of God.

I believe that the high level of commitment we see in the Muslim people towards Islam is something that Christians can learn from. I also believe that it is possible for those who were committed to their faith in Islam to be and are becoming just as committed to their new faith in Jesus Christ, in just the same way that Paul became committed to spreading the gospel having been so vehemently opposed to it. At first Paul was committed to Judaism and was a fierce opponent of the gospel. But when he met Jesus on the road to Damascus, his life was completely turned around and he became fully committed to sharing the gospel, particularly with the Gentile world.

My message to the church in the West is that we are one body. We need you as much as you need us. It is very comfortable to live in the West as a Christian but it is very uncomfortable to live as a Christian here in the Middle East. Therefore you need this push from us to encourage you to stay on the right track. At the same time we need your prayers, your support, and your love and care. The most important thing for us is to know that there are Christians who are praying for us and visiting us and caring for us. Palestinian Christians do not feel that they are cared for. When I go to Gaza and meet with the Christians there, they receive me so warmly because they appreciate being visited. And it is the same with the Palestinian Christians living in the West Bank: they feel forgotten and alone. Please remember that there are Palestinian Christians as well as Messianic Jewish people living in this land, and we are one body.

CHAPTER 9

Tzachi Danor – a Moroccan Jew Becomes a Missionary with Jews for Jesus

For 2,000 years, several Arab nations provided a safe haven for the Jewish diaspora, including Morocco. But in 1948, when Israel declared her sovereignty and was reborn as a nation, the Arab nations that immediately surrounded Israel declared war on the infant state. Since then, things have never been the same.

In Israel today you will find Jews from many Arab or Muslim countries – Yemen, Iraq, Iran, Syria, Tunisia, Egypt, Algeria, Libya, Lebanon, Turkey, and Morocco. Some are Sephardi Jews (Jews who settled and formed communities in Spain, Portugal, North Africa, and the Middle East) while others are Mizrahi Jews (or eastern Jews; descendants of Jewish immigrants from the eastern Arab or Muslim countries).

Since 1948, approximately 850,000 Jews have immigrated to Israel from these Arab nations. Prior to this time, half lived in the French-controlled Maghreb region (which included the Atlas Mountains and the coastal plains of Morocco, Algeria, Tunisia, and Libya), 15 to 20 per cent in Iraq, 10 per cent in Egypt, 7 per cent in Yemen, and 25 per cent lived in Iran and Turkey.

From 1944 the Jewish leadership in Palestine encouraged the immigration to Israel of all the Jews living in Arab and Muslim countries in what was called the One Million Plan. The first exodus occurred in the late 1940s and early 1950s, when over 90 per cent of Jews from Iraq, Yemen, and Libya opted to leave their property behind and start a new life in what was soon to become the State of Israel. A further 260,000 Jews from other Arab countries immigrated to Israel between 1948 and 1951 and accounted for 56 per cent of the total immigration to the newly founded state.

Many Jews living in Egypt moved to Israel in 1956 following the Suez Crisis. Immigration of Jews from the Maghreb countries reached its climax during the 1960s. Six hundred thousand Jews from Arab and Muslim countries had reached Israel by 1972. By the 1980s, 80 per cent of Iranian Jews had left the country and moved to Israel.

The reasons for the exodus of these Jewish communities is much argued over by historians, depending on their view and version of history, and much politicized. But for the purposes of this book, when asking the question, "What is God doing in Israel?", we have to consider the biblical prophecies that refer to these events. For example, we read in Isaiah,

**In that day the Lord will reach out his hand a
second time to reclaim the remnant that is left of
his people from Assyria [Iraq, Syria, Jordan, and
Lebanon], from Lower Egypt, from Upper Egypt,
from Cush [Ethiopia], from Elam [Iran], from
Babylonia [Iraq], from Hamath [Beka'a Valley in
Lebanon] and from the islands of the sea.**

**He will raise a banner for the nations
and gather the exiles of Israel;
he will assemble the scattered people of Judah
from the four quarters of the earth.**[59]

Did God use persecution, anti-Semitism, and even the
Holocaust to encourage the Jewish exodus from these
countries?

To understand Tzachi Danor's story we have to first
understand a little of his background. His parents were
both born into Jewish families in Morocco.

Jews began emigrating to Morocco from Israel as early
as AD 70, after the Romans sacked Jerusalem. Morocco
provided a safe haven for Jewish people for centuries,
along with Tunisia and Algeria; here they did not suffer
persecution or expulsion. By the 1940s, Morocco's Jewish
population had reached its peak and exceeded 250,000
people.

During the Second World War, however (while
Morocco was still a French Protectorate), the Vichy
government in France passed laws against the Jewish
community that prevented them from obtaining credit. If
Jews lived or had businesses in European neighbourhoods

they were expelled, and only 2 per cent of the jobs in law and medicine were allowed to be taken by Jewish people. However, the then king of Morocco, King Mohammed V, did not approve of these laws and promised the Moroccan Jewish leaders that he would never harm Jewish people or their property.

In 1948, however, during the first Arab–Israeli war, violent anti-Jewish riots occurred in Oujda and Djerada, and forty-four Jews lost their lives. It was after these events that 18,000 Moroccan Jews left the country.

When Morocco gained independence in 1956, Jews who had held several senior political positions were not reappointed. As Morocco began to identify more closely with the Arab and Muslim world, the Jewish community became fearful. Subsequently, by 1956 more than 25,000 Moroccan Jews had left. Not all went to Israel; many went to France, Belgium, Spain, or Canada. Those who went to Israel formed the second-largest Jewish community (approximately a million people) after the Russian Jews.

It is against this backdrop that we now consider Tzachi's story. I first met him in February 2012 in Tel Aviv at the headquarters of Jews for Jesus,[60] where he was working as a missionary. His story encapsulates the essence of this book because not only here is a man whose family have made aliyah to Israel, but also here is a man who has discovered that Jesus is the Messiah of Israel and understands that he has a part to play in the unfolding story of what God is doing there today.

Tzachi was born in Akko (Acre), a city on the shores of the Mediterranean in northern Israel, close to the border with Lebanon. This city is one of the oldest continuously inhabited cities in the world with a history reaching back to Pharaoh Thutmose III – 1504 to 1450 BC. Today, Akko is home to a population of approximately 40,000 people, Jews and Arabs. Throughout the 1950s many Jewish neighbourhoods were established around the city to provide homes for the numerous Jewish immigrants who were arriving, the vast majority being Jews from Morocco.

My first impression of Tzachi was of a warm, outgoing, friendly person. He was keen to share his story, which he did with great humour and lack of self-pity, despite recalling memories of sad times during his childhood.

I was born in Akko in 1977. I am a Moroccan Jew. Both my parents were born in Morocco. I grew up with no father because my parents separated when I was one year old (although their divorce would not be finalized for another twenty years). My mother and I lived with my grandmother until I was seven, and then we lived alone.

I saw my father for the first time in my life when I was in the army and he returned from overseas to live in Israel again. We spent four hours together. He was a stranger to me then and remained a stranger; I really do not know my father at all. My mother was for me both a mother and a father and I am her only child.

I grew up in Akko and my childhood was not easy because of the family situation and my father not being there. But on the other hand I had a big family on my mother's side because she is the youngest of eight children, so I was surrounded by a very warm, mostly secular Jewish family. However, my grandmother and some of my aunts and uncles attended synagogue weekly. Although most were not outwardly religious, they followed God in their minds and customs. They believed in God and prayed to Him but they had no knowledge of the Bible and knew nothing about Yeshua or the New Testament. They only knew what they heard from the rabbis when they went to the synagogue.

At school I was taught about the oral law[61] and a little from the Tenach (Old Testament). Israeli schools do not teach from the New Testament, so all we were taught was either from the Tenach or from the oral law.

Following my Bar Mitzvah[62] at the age of thirteen, I loved to go to the synagogue and felt very drawn to the religious world and to prayer. This was my connection to God. I never heard about Yeshua during my childhood or when I was a teenager. None of my friends were Christian and I didn't know any Jewish people who believed in Yeshua. So until the age of twenty-four my connection to God was through the synagogue and Judaism. I prayed and felt connected to God, and this is how I knew Him.

After serving my time in the army, I took a job in order to save enough money to leave Israel and travel around the world. I decided to go to America where many of my relatives lived. In summer 2001, aged twenty-four, I arrived in Dallas, Texas. I had a long list of plans for how I would get rich and be able to buy all the things that I would like to own, and to marry an

American woman in order to live in the USA! I went to a synagogue in Dallas and got to know the rabbi there very well; in fact, I informally became known as his "right-hand man". I would open the synagogue every morning, participate in the prayer, and wear the tallit[63] and tefillin.[64]

At first my time in Dallas was very successful. I felt settled, especially at the synagogue, and I had a job and a car and I was looking for a wife! But one year later my whole life changed when, through my job, I met a Jewish American woman called Rebecca. She was the one who first told me about Yeshua and introduced me to the whole Bible – the Old and the New Testaments. She began to show me the prophecies in the Old Testament concerning Yeshua and how they were fulfilled in the New Testament. I was shocked and surprised because I didn't understand that if Yeshua was in the Tenach, if He came from the Jewish book, then how come He is not talked about in the synagogues? Why is He not mentioned in the Jewish prayers? Why do the rabbis not talk about Him?

I had many questions back then, and as I continued to study and attend meetings with Rebecca, she and her friends organized a special Bible study for me every day after work. Slowly I started to understand the Scriptures, and at the same time I realized that in religious Jewish circles, talking about Yeshua was not popular, as Orthodox Jews did not believe in Him.

As I continued to study the Bible with Rebecca and her friends, I started to wonder what direction my life would take from now on. If I started to believe in Yeshua, how could I tell my rabbi and how could I tell my mother in Israel? Learning about Yeshua was a totally new thing for me. Because I had never heard about Him before, I had no opinions or prejudices, unlike many Israelis who consider Yeshua to be the cause of so much Jewish misery and persecution.

When I talk to Israelis on the streets of Tel Aviv today, I hear their views about Yeshua, or Jesus, being the Gentile God and how Jews have been mocked and scorned throughout history by Christians and blamed for the death of Jesus on the cross. But because I had never heard such opinions, all this was new to me.

I studied the Bible with Rebecca and her friends for a year and gradually I began to realize that what they were teaching me about Yeshua, from both the Old and New Testaments, was true. Still, I felt that this faith was only for Jews from the diaspora and the Gentiles; I didn't need it because I was born in Israel and had the rabbis to follow. It was only after I had a personal encounter with Yeshua during the Passover in 2003 that I realized my need to put my own faith in Him.

When I returned to Israel in 2003 I encountered the most difficult time of my life, not because of my faith that Yeshua was our Messiah, but because my mother was very unwell with cancer. I was her only child, I had been away for almost three years, and I had come back as a new believer to find my mother seriously ill. I didn't have a job. But perhaps the most difficult thing was that I didn't know any other believers in Israel. I felt very alone and didn't know what to do with my new faith. Where should I go? Who should I talk to?

Before I left America, my rabbi told me that I would face many troubles in Israel from the Orthodox Jews and non-believers because of my belief in Yeshua. However, I soon discovered that God had all these matters in hand, and it wasn't long before a brother from a Messianic congregation near to Akko contacted me and came to my home and introduced himself and took me to his congregation on Shabbat. That way I began to get to know the body of Messiah in Israel.

In 2004 my mother was still very ill. I shared with her how I had come to believe in Yeshua and I showed her the Scriptures about Him. I bought her a Bible and together we began to read about Yeshua and how, when He was on earth, He healed many sick people and performed many miracles. In the beginning she was interested, but whether it was because of the treatment she was undergoing, she dropped the subject. I, on the other hand, continued with my faith.

In 2005 I went back to America for another year, and on returning to Israel during the winter of 2006 I started to pray and ask God about my future and what He wanted me to do now. I had worked as a volunteer with Jews for Jesus in Tel Aviv for two years during 2004 and 2005 and got to know the staff well. At that time they had tried to persuade me to join the team, but I decided that the time wasn't right. However, by the summer of 2007, I knew that this was the type of work I wanted to do for God – to go on to the streets and tell people the truth; talk to those who didn't yet know the truth about Yeshua.

Joining the Jews for Jesus team in Tel Aviv in 2007 was the prelude to meeting my wife, Sarah, the following year. We were both participating in the Jews for Jesus Behold Your God (BYG) campaign in Tel Aviv that year. This was my first year with the ministry and I was very excited. The campaign officially started with a Passover Seder (meal) at the Hotel Gilgal in Tel Aviv, where I broke a forty-day fast. You see, I was finishing forty days of fasting and prayer seeking God's favour for a successful campaign... and for finding a wife!

Sarah's story ...

Although, like Tzachi, Sarah is Jewish, her story is very different from Tzachi's. Sarah grew up in New Jersey in the United States of America and her parents, Leonard and Esther Galiley, are both believers in Yeshua (Jesus). On her mother's side, Sarah is a descendant of multiple generations of Jewish believers and missionaries. She says:

I grew up primarily in a Protestant worship environment, but since my grandparents led a Jewish mission called "Messengers of the New Covenant" in New Jersey, they were instrumental in imparting to us grandchildren our identity as Jewish believers in Jesus.

My great-grandparents were Russian-speaking Jews who lived in Odessa. My great-grandfather, Julius, worked for a Christian cabinet-maker who showed him the Old Testament prophecies concerning Messiah and explained how Yeshua had fulfilled them all. Julius saw that Jesus was indeed the Jewish Messiah, and prayed to receive Him into his life. Normally a quiet man, Julius became quite animated and bold in sharing the gospel with his family, friends, and neighbours.

Later, Julius and his wife moved to Istanbul and it was there that my grandfather, Isaac Finestone, was born. I remember him fondly. He had an old-world, measured dignity, even in interacting with his grandchildren, reflecting his Eastern European Chassidic roots. Although he lived in North America most of his adult life, he always spoke with a distinct Yiddish accent.

My grandparents' home was an important place for me when I was growing up; it was a place where I learned about my Jewish identity and about the value of family. I remember their home's decor reflected a twentieth-century Jewish aesthetic and was accented with Judaica from Israel and my grandfather's voluminous book collection. When we visited on Passover, the home was filled with the scents of my grandmother Ivy's Passover cooking, including her legendary sponge cake which few can duplicate, even with her recipe.

Isaac and Ivy lived an adventurous life. In 1967, they decided to move to Israel. They settled for a time in Netanya and were there during the Six-Day War. Owing to Isaac's failing health, they returned to the US after about a year and Isaac passed away in 1970, shortly after their return. At that point, Ivy moved into an apartment on the top floor of my parents' home.

My grandmother was a significant spiritual influence on me and my brother and sister. She was a marvellous storyteller and she prayed with us and read to us. Most of the gifts she gave us were spiritual books. Since she had a small apartment on the third floor of our home, we could go up to visit her often and would frequently find her lying on her bed with her arms raised to heaven praying audibly for us. She led a rich and thrilling life of faith in God from her childhood in British Columbia, Canada, and was an inspiring, godly example to me.

I clearly remember the day I prayed to receive Yeshua at the age of eight. My dad was watching Billy Graham preaching on television and he decided he wanted us children to watch also. At the end, many people in the stadium where he was preaching began walking forward in response to his message. My dad excitedly pointed out many young people who were among the crowd coming forward and asked if I also wanted to pray to accept Jesus as my Saviour. To be honest, I felt a bit odd and resistant, but in my heart I knew it was always right to say "yes" to God, so I agreed to pray with my dad. Since I came to faith at a young age under parental influence, throughout my life it has been necessary for me to reaffirm this decision and rededicate my heart to the Lord at various points. I have gone through many times of trial and sadness, but each time I have said "yes" to God, He has brought me further in spiritual maturity and has never failed me.

After finishing high school, I moved to North Carolina, and attended Davidson College and earned a Bachelor's degree in English literature. I also spent part of one summer in New York City where I participated in Chosen People Ministries' Summer Training and Evangelism (STEP) programme, continuing the tradition of Jewish ministry started by my grandparents. Although at that time I did not anticipate becoming a full-time missionary, I had an experience that made me rethink the purposes of God in my life.

I first met my cousin Martha Brickner Jacobs (sister of David Brickner, the current executive director of Jews for Jesus) when I was in college. Martha and her husband Loren were working for Jews for Jesus in New York City. When they moved to Michigan, Loren invited me to consider coming to work with them in their ministry, "Shema Yisrael", but I declined.

Sometime later, I had a dream that I was visiting Martha and Loren in their new home in Michigan and Loren was asking me again to come and work with them. After praying and talking to them, I felt that God was leading me to join them. I packed my car and moved to Michigan, where I worked with them for about two years. Martha and Loren nurtured me and encouraged me in thousands of ways, and it was an amazing season of growing and developing spiritually and learning about the life of ministry.

After this, I returned to New Jersey and began working as an instructional aide in a school for children with autism. I attended New Jersey City University where I earned an MA in Special Education. I became a full-time special education teacher. Working with children with autism was an amazingly illuminating experience that taught me a lot in general about human behaviour and motivation and how to be a positive influence on others.

During this time, I used my summer vacations to participate in various ministry projects. I went to Argentina and to Siberia with Jewish Voice Ministries and led the intercessory prayer team for a Jews for Jesus campaign in New Jersey.

In 2007, I resigned from my teaching position in response to a strong spiritual impression that God had something new for me. I was praying about assuming a new role in the school the following year when the Lord clearly directed me to resign! I was surprised, but I obeyed by faith, to the surprise of my colleagues. I continued to pray about the next step as the summer vacation began. It was then that Josh Sofaer, who was the director of Jews for Jesus' New York branch and a member of my congregation in New Jersey, suggested that I consider working with Jews for Jesus. In my mind I dismissed the idea right away, certain that I wasn't cut out for street evangelism Jews for Jesus style, but within a month, the Lord made it very clear to me while I was on a spiritual retreat that this was exactly what He wanted me to do!

I took a temporary administrative job with the ministry, while continuing to do evangelistic campaigns. In 2008, I flew to Israel to participate in the Behold Your God (BYG) outreach in Tel Aviv. It was there I met Tzachi, who had recently become a missionary with Jews for Jesus.

Tzachi remembers that day …

At the Passover Seder (meal) at the Hotel Gilgal in Tel Aviv where I broke a forty-day fast I can honestly say I was completely focused on the start of the campaign – I was not expecting to meet my wife!

Right after we finished the BYG Tel Aviv campaign, we participated in another three-week campaign in London, England. One evening, I asked Sarah to pray with me for the success of the outreach. I saw that she was mature spiritually by the way she worshipped. We walked to a park and sat on a bench and started to talk about our lives. Because of her spiritual maturity, I told Sarah I had noticed that there was something different about her, something special, and I told her that I wanted a wife like her!

Tzachi and Sarah soon realized that God had brought them together, and they were married in August 2009. Since then, Sarah has joined Tzachi in sharing the gospel with the people of Israel. While she continues to participate in evangelistic campaigns and other street evangelism opportunities, Sarah's favourite part of being a missionary is meeting with people one to one.

I love teaching the Bible on visits, making connections between Old and New Testament events and ideas. I like to give a multidimensional historical perspective on the passages I teach whenever I can. I also particularly like to reach out to the elderly. They have a lot of wisdom and life experience and their place in life makes them naturally contemplate eternal things seriously.

Tzachi reflects …

When we go out on to the streets of Tel Aviv and hand out tracts and talk to people about Yeshua, we get all kinds of reactions. Some people are very open to listen to what we have to say while others are extremely hostile towards us. We face all kinds of situations. Some people ask us to pray with them right there on the streets or in the coffee shops; after hearing about Yeshua they want to give their lives to Him right away. We also face strong opposition, mostly from the religious Orthodox Jews who try to prevent us from talking to people. But despite this often vehement opposition, we remain strong because we know we have the truth for them. We try to persuade them to be more open minded and be prepared to look at the Bible and read what it has to say about Yeshua. I tell them my story of how somebody showed me a Bible in Dallas and I read for myself about Yeshua, how His coming was prophesied and how those prophecies were fulfilled.

Recently I was talking to a man I had met earlier on the streets. We had sent him a book and I called him to ask if he would like to meet and talk further. He was an 87-year-old Israeli living close to Tel Aviv, and he wanted to hear more about Jesus. We arranged a date and I went to visit him. As we talked, I discovered that he had read both the Old and New Testaments and knew a lot about Jesus, but he hadn't taken the step of giving his life to Jesus and embracing Him as his Saviour. I asked him if he would like to know Jesus personally, if he would like to invite Him into his heart, and he said yes. So I led him in prayer and now we meet every two weeks to study the Bible together. He is elderly, he lives alone, and he has no family.

To go and reach the lost sheep of the house of Israel is our call at Jews for Jesus. This is what energizes us every day and encourages us to put on our Jews for Jesus T-shirts and get out on the streets to tell people about Yeshua, or to visit people in their homes and study the Bible together. I love this work, which is my call from God.

CHAPTER 10

Shmuel Salway – an Indian Jew Who Finds Yeshua

Come with me to Tel Aviv to meet a Jewish man whose family came to Israel from India! His name is Shmuel Salway. He is the associate pastor of a Messianic congregation called Adonai Roi ("Adonai Roi" means the Lord is my shepherd, from Psalm 23). As with so many Jewish people, he has a fascinating, although at times painful, story to tell.

Shmuel has travelled the world but was drawn back to Israel by a strong sense of being called there by God. At first he did not know the reason why. But today he has discovered his destiny and his life is full of a sense of purpose that drives him on in the face of great challenges. He firmly believes that God is central to what is happening in Israel and the wider Middle East today, as he goes on to describe. But first he tells the story of the Jewish diaspora that developed over the centuries in India.

My parents were Indian Jews who immigrated to Israel in the early 1960s. I was born and raised here in Israel.

There is a long history of Jewish people living in India. There are several Indian Jewish communities in India. My mother came from Pune in central India, close to Bombay, where the Jewish community maintained their Jewish identity throughout the centuries. I was able to visit there a few years ago and I saw a Torah scroll that was several hundred years old. I was able to research which synagogue my grandfather belonged to and I saw his name inscribed there.

Most of the Jews in India have now immigrated to Israel, but the ancient synagogues are still there. They are not as splendid as they used to be and you have to use your imagination as to how they would once have looked because now there is nobody left to care for them, so they are falling into disrepair.

There were two main migrations of India's Jews to Israel; the first in the early 1950s and the second in the 1960s. My mum came in the 1960s with her family, along with many others from their community. Today there are approximately 40,000 Indian Jews living in Israel.

During the exile it was very important for Jewish people to maintain their Jewish identity and they had to fight to keep the Torah and the Shabbat and to marry within their faith. When they came to Israel they brought their very strict Jewish rules with them. They were not outwardly religious in the dress sense but they were very conservative Jews.

My mother came to faith in Yeshua in a Messianic congregation in Jaffa, Tel Aviv. Her family, who were very conservative, were extremely opposed to her new faith. They did not understand what it meant to be a Messianic Jew. They thought she had converted to Christianity and become a Christian. She had been taught to stay away from Christians and if anybody veered from that rule, the threat if you converted to any other religion (which in India included Hinduism, Christianity, or Islam), was that you would be disowned by your family. So when my mother started to believe in Yeshua the family decided to disown her. Her father told her she was as good as dead to them and they wanted nothing more to do with her. Nobody in her family was allowed to talk to anybody in our family (I have three sisters). We have cousins who live less than an hour's drive away, but to this day we have never met.

My grandfather passed away a few years ago and I went with my mother to support her at his funeral. She had not been invited to attend but she had heard about his death and wanted to pay her last respects at the graveside. I watched my grandma in tears as she walked past us without acknowledging our presence. My aunts, uncles, and cousins all ignored us; they didn't even say hello to my mum. It was very painful for her. It was painful for me and I didn't know them, so you can imagine how much more painful it was for my mother. She had decided to follow Yeshua, and being ostracized by her family was a sacrifice she had been willing to make.

When I was growing up I didn't really care about God. Tel Aviv is a very secular city. I was more interested in school and studies and sports, and I never thought about making a commitment to Yeshua.

When I was sixteen years old I was invited to a conference that was being organized by a Messianic congregation. I don't remember exactly what the guest speaker spoke about but it was a challenging message, and when he invited people who wanted to give their life to Yeshua to come forward, I resisted with all my strength! I was at the back of the room. I had only gone there to meet some friends. There was no way I was going to go forward – I was too cool for that! But when the speaker encouraged people to go forward I found myself so challenged that I hung on to the chair in order not to move! I stayed rooted to my chair, and once the conference was over I breathed a sigh of relief and ran outside. I told myself that if that was God, then I did not want to know Him and I did not need Him.

When I reached home later that night I went straight to bed. I pulled the covers over my head and found myself weeping. Now I am a young Israeli man and we don't usually cry that easily! But I was weeping because I knew that God had touched my life. I asked Him to forgive me, and that was the start of my relationship with Yeshua. As I thought about this experience, I realized that there must be something truly significant about believing in Him. I thought about my mother and how much she had been prepared to suffer and be rejected by her parents and family when she came to faith. I knew my mother would not have given up so much if God was just an idea or a concept; there had to be something much more.

I started reading the New Testament to find out why people were prepared to change their lives in order to believe. I had to find out for myself that God was real. My mum's experience had challenged me, but even so, I had to discover my own path to faith.

At the age of eighteen, like the majority of people in Israel, I joined the Israel Defense Forces (IDF). Boys have to serve a minimum of three years, and girls two years. I was a combat medic in Lebanon.

In Israel, many summer camps take place when groups of children go camping in the country. We are surrounded by nations that are not very friendly towards us, so on trips involving children and young people we need armed escorts and a medic in case a child is injured. Being a combat medic I had both a gun and medical training, so I was ideally suited to escort such camping trips. As a young man in the army I wasn't really on fire for God. I deliberately kept quiet about my faith; it was a private matter between me and God.

One summer I was asked to be a counsellor at a youth camp for children from Messianic congregations across Israel. The young people would come and talk to me and ask me questions about a wide range of topics. Often the questions involved boy- or girlfriends. One time I was asked, "I have a boyfriend but he is not a believer in Yeshua – is that OK?" My immediate response was to say that it was not a wise thing because of what the Bible had to say on the subject, not knowing exactly where in the Bible I could find such advice! I would go home from camp and read some books in order to be better prepared for the next time. But I could not keep up with their questions! One child shared with me that one of his parents had died and as they had not believed in Yeshua would they be in heaven?

During this time I was challenged to know more about what the Bible had to say on such matters because children want to know the truth, and they are quick to realize if what you are saying is not genuine. It was then that I really decided to commit my life to the Lord wholeheartedly and live the life of a believer, to know what the Bible has to say about these deep questions of life and death, to hear from God, and to have a close relationship with Him.

After finishing my army service I began my studies at Tel Aviv University before moving on to study at the Hebrew University in Jerusalem. Then for a few years I worked for the Airport Authority before accepting a job with ElAl, the Israeli airline, in New York City. I lived in Manhattan and worked for both ElAl and the Israeli Consulate where, as a security officer, I was involved in various missions. But I always knew my calling was to come back to the land of Israel and serve God.

I stayed in New York for three years to fulfil my initial contract, fully expecting to return to Israel after that time. But I was offered an extension to my contract which enabled me to stay for a further four years. This was rare, and during this time I always knew that God eventually wanted me back in Israel to work among young people. It was a tussle, however: I was happy working in New York, but the draw to return to Israel just would not go away.

When I did eventually return four years later, I found a Messianic congregation in Tel Aviv called Adonai

Roi,[65] led by a pastor called Avi Mizrachi. I really felt at home there and after a short while, Avi had a chat with me to say he had heard about my work with young people over the years, and as the youth pastor at Adonai Roi had just left, would I be willing to take on this volunteer role. After a few months of working with the young people, Avi spoke to me again and invited me to join the team as a member of staff! I knew this was God's best plan for my life so I readily agreed, and that is how I came to be a full-time staff member of Dugit, an evangelistic outreach centre in the heart of Tel Aviv, staffed by Adonai Roi members and directed by Avi Mizrachi. Dugit, which means little fishing boats, started in 1993.

I have to be honest and admit that I struggled with giving up a well-paid job in America to return to Israel and be prepared to work within a congregation. It took me a while to put my own desires and ambitions to one side, and I can remember having many "conversations" with God, asking Him to confirm very clearly that I was making right decisions.

I had asked God for my job in New York as a security supervisor, and God made that possible. I had also asked Him to give me the opportunity to travel around the world before returning to Israel. Working for an airline enabled me to do this. I visited such places as Africa, Australia, New Zealand, South America, and Asia. I had wanted to have the experience of living in a foreign country and God allowed me to do this, but I always knew He wanted me back in Israel.

I met my wife when I returned to Israel. She was a youth leader with another congregation in Tel Aviv. It was during an event when all the youth groups in the city met together that we met each other. So in being obedient in coming back to the land and working with teenagers and young adults, I also met my wife Susie. She is a Sabra (a native-born Israeli), and today we have three young children!

After seven years working as the youth pastor, Shmuel was made the associate pastor at Adonai Roi. He is responsible for overseeing the smooth running of the Dugit office as well as preparing sermons and services for the congregation on Shabbat. He still meets with the youth each week as well as with several young couples, as the congregation is predominantly made up of young people.

Our vision is to preach the gospel and make disciples. In the coffee shop we hold live music events and regularly talk to people about Yeshua. People hear the music and are curious to know who we are and what we stand for. So they come in and we have many meaningful conversations in this way.

We also run a food and clothing distribution service. We receive the names of poor people from the city's Department of Social Affairs. They don't believe in Yeshua, but when they come and meet us and find out why we do what we do, they are interested to know more about the Bible and what it has to say about Yeshua. We are here to help, so whether we give out bags of clothes or bags of food, we are able to practically share the love of Yeshua with them.

In our country, the older generation have been taught to stay away from the New Testament, Christians, and Christianity because of the historical connection between Christianity and the persecution of Jewish people through the centuries leading up to the Holocaust. But we find that younger people today are more open. They are interested in the New Age movement and Scientology so they are willing to hear about Yeshua and to take a New Testament. A few years ago this would not have been the case; things have changed a great deal here in Israel and there is a new openness to discuss frankly about Jesus. More recently there have been a number of radio and television programmes about Yeshua and the Messianic Jewish movement in the land, including interviews with a number of Messianic Jewish believers. So with this media exposure, awareness of our existence has increased, and as a result our numbers have increased.

When I look at the situation here today, I can see that God is moving powerfully in this land. People are more open than ever before to hearing about Yeshua. Twenty years ago there were only a handful of believers in the land. Today there are congregations throughout the country. Here in Tel Aviv there are at least eight Messianic Hebrew-speaking congregations. Currently in our weekly home group there are two or three secular Israelis who come because they are interested. The harvest is ready but the labourers are few, so we are praying for more Jews to become believers and leaders in the land.

Growing up in Israel as an Israeli Jew, I became aware that many countries boycott Israeli goods and criticize Israel unfairly, but I did not understand the reasons why. Why is the world against us, I would wonder? Why are we surrounded by so many enemies who want to annihilate us? It's not as though we have vast oil reserves or rich mineral deposits; indeed, many of the countries surrounding us who are against us have far greater natural resources than Israel. These are the questions many Israeli Jews ask who are not believers and who have no understanding of the Bible or spiritual matters. We are a tiny country. So it's not a matter of size. There is therefore no logical way to understand this hostility towards us.

I have come to realize that the only way you can understand it is by understanding God and looking at it spiritually. Spiritually, I believe God has a unique calling on the Jewish people, and God prophesied that Jews would come back to the land,[66] and they are coming back to the land from the four corners of the earth. But not only that, God also prophesied that He would be their God and they would be His people,[67] and that can only happen after a time of repentance and recognizing the sacrifice of Yeshua who died for our sins. Therefore I believe God intends to save the Jewish people as well as the Gentile people. Just before He died, when Jesus was in Jerusalem, He wept over the city:

"Jerusalem, Jerusalem, you who kill the prophets
and stone those sent to you, how often I have
longed to gather your children together, as a hen
gathers her chicks under her wings, but you were
not willing."[68]

Jesus here was talking to the Jewish people. He wasn't talking to the Roman soldiers or the Gentiles. Rather He was looking at the Jewish people and accusing them of being disbelieving and obstinate. How many times I called you – I wanted to gather you – but you would not listen to me. Jesus told them that they would not see Him again until they cried, "Baruch Haba B'Shem Adonai,"[69] which means, "Blessed is he who comes in the name of the Lord."

If you look at it spiritually, the enemy knows that Jesus will return when Jewish people start calling for the Messiah. But if Satan can manage to wipe out Israel and kill the Jewish people, then God's prophecies will not be able to be fulfilled.

Throughout history we can see that this is what the enemy has tried to do many times. The Holocaust is a recent example of this; the enemy caused this to happen, not God. The enemy tried to kill the Jewish people, to wipe them off the face of the earth. But God was merciful and, despite the Holocaust, we are back in the land in our own country, just as God promised.

But the enemy has not given up in his attempts to prevent the Jewish people from recognizing Yeshua, Jesus, as their Messiah. The majority of Jewish people are not aware that Yeshua is their Messiah at present, but I believe this will happen. The prayers of the saints around the world on behalf of Israel and the Jewish people are heard by God, and there is definitely more openness today throughout Israel to the gospel.

We have to ask what goes through the minds of Jewish people when they come to Israel from the four corners of the world, often having left behind what little they owned, only to realize that much of the world hates them and wants to destroy them. It is difficult to understand unless you see it through spiritual eyes. My family came here from India. They immigrated with very little. They were unable to sell their land and came to Israel with only the possessions they could fit into their suitcase, leaving everything else behind.

My wife's parents came to Israel from Morocco and Iraq respectively, and her father (who came from Morocco) left his estate there and arrived in Israel with nothing. Life was hard for those early settlers; not only did they have to clear the land (much of it was swampy), but they also had to fight repeated wars from neighbouring nations who wanted to drive them out. The sacrifice those people made was immense. But God prophesied that He would bring people from the north, from the east, and the west, and the south.[70] If they had only come from the north or from Europe in the west, that would not have been enough. If they had just come from the south, that would not have been a complete fulfilment of that prophecy. They had to come from the four corners – the Ethiopian Jews from Africa, the Jews from India and China, Europe, and America.

While we are sorry to see that anti-Semitic behaviour has become more widespread in recent times, I believe the only way Jews will come back to this land is when life becomes too uncomfortable for them where they are. In America, which is home to the biggest population of Jews outside of Israel, most are reluctant to immigrate to a country where life will be hard. I hope it doesn't, but I believe persecution will arise in America, and Jewish people will then be more likely to come to live in Israel.

What happened in France in January 2015 when four Jewish people were murdered in a Jewish supermarket in Paris following the attack and subsequent killing of twelve journalists at the Charlie Hebdo offices is, I believe, symptomatic of what will happen in other countries. The signs are there. There is an increase in violence towards Jewish people. When the Israeli president visited France after the attack, he encouraged Jewish people to come to Israel – only there would they feel safe, he told them. As a result, many French Jews are making aliyah.

Persecution of Messianic Jews, however, comes mainly from Jewish people. The majority of Jewish people do not understand Messianic Judaism. They understand Christianity as the religion that has persecuted them through the centuries. As far as the average Jew is concerned, the Crusaders were Christians who came and killed Jews in the name of Jesus.

For many, when they do read the New Testament, their comment is that they never realized it was a Jewish book or that Yeshua was Jewish. It is a revelation to them when they discover that He talked about Shabbat; He was called Rabbi; He talked about the Law and the Commandments. He didn't start a different religion with Christian rituals. Rather, He taught them how they could be fulfilled Jews; how they could be Jews who believed in the God of Israel and the Messiah, Yeshua Jesus.

If you ask me what God is doing here in Israel today, I can see Jews are returning as a result of prophecy being fulfilled, and what we can expect to see happen next is vividly revealed in the prophecy of Ezekiel. If you look at the prophecy in Ezekiel that talks about dry bones,[71] it says:

> "This is what the Sovereign Lord says to these bones: I will make breath enter you, and you will come to life … Then you will know that I am the Lord."

That is the first part of the prophecy. It goes on to say:

> "I will put my Spirit in you and you will live."

That can only happen through a relationship with Yeshua Jesus.

Yes, Jews are still coming back to the land, but meanwhile I believe we will start to see Jews asking what it means to be Jewish. They will search for God, and in searching for God they will find their Messiah. I pray that God will send more workers to bring this harvest in. I pray for the peace of Jerusalem, that the true peace can be found – Yeshua, the Prince of Peace.

It is also important that we have a correct understanding of how God sees the Israeli Arabs and Palestinians living in Israel and the wider Middle East. For many, their families have lived in this land for generations. There are many Israeli Arab Christians who have a heart for Israel and who want to share in fellowship with Messianic Jewish believers and Muslim-background believers (MBBs) living in the West Bank. They believe that they too have a part to play in God's plan for Israel and the nations of the world at this time, and that is our understanding of the Word of God too!

We have a sister congregation in Jaffa that is comprised of Arab Christians. We often meet together. We also meet regularly to pray. Just last week there was a gathering of women – Christian Arabs and Messianic Jewish believers – led by Chaya Mizrachi, our pastor Avi's wife. Such meetings are happening regularly now. We believe in reconciliation, but not on the basis of politics or questions regarding ownership of the land. Rather, we understand that we are one in Messiah, in Yeshua, and have a genuine love and concern for one another. We experience peace together because of what Yeshua, the Prince of Peace, has done for us. We pray for our Palestinian brothers in the West Bank, especially those who are Muslims, that they too would come to enjoy knowing Jesus, Yeshua. It is not easy for them because Islam is very strong in the West Bank, and to believe in Jesus brings persecution.

We are hearing about and starting to meet Muslim-background believers; this is a recent development. At the same time, Jewish people are coming to Israel from around the world. Jewish people are coming to know their Messiah. Muslim people are coming to know the Messiah. Perhaps the picture is bigger than we first imagined. We have to learn to read the signs. We have to look around at what is going on in the world. We look at the local situation and see a lot of trouble. But look further and we see prophecies are being fulfilled. Therefore we believe Yeshua will be returning soon. In the coming days we are expecting to hear many more testimonies of people coming to know Yeshua. We also know this will lead to more persecution. By following what is going on here in Israel we can see God's plans unfolding.

We are based in downtown Tel Aviv. Some people call Israel the Holy Land, but Tel Aviv is an extremely secular and liberal city and far from being holy. Tel Aviv is called the "white city" because the buildings are white. But Tel Aviv is the centre for much ungodly behaviour and dark spiritual activity within Israel. It seems to us that the enemy is working overtime here and in Jerusalem and across Israel, trying to take Jewish people away from their calling to be a light to the nations.[72] It seems to us that many Jewish people are going further and further away from God in their search for Him. It says in the Bible that,

> They are zealous for God but, their zeal is not
> based on knowledge.[73]

They are looking for God, but in the wrong places. They are looking at different religions or pleasures of the world for their fulfilment. But they will eventually reach the point when they realize they can never be fulfilled by the world but only through their relationship with God through Yeshua Jesus. I believe God created humanity in such a way that ultimate fulfilment can only be achieved when we know Him.

Young people in Israel are trying to be like young people around the world. They are looking for success and trying to find ways to become rich. How can they be like the celebrities they see on the television? But underneath it all, when I talk to them, I think what they are really seeking is their calling. When they hear about Yeshua and start to read the Bible, they are challenged. They start to ask about their purpose for being in the land, and ask about their calling. The temptation for them is to be like the rest of the world. There are many distractions for them.

For centuries there has been a veil over Jewish eyes. But that is changing. My wife's family and my mother's family were all warned to stay away from the New Testament because it was considered to be a pagan, foreign book which has nothing to do with our faith in the God of Israel. But now there is an unveiling of the eyes; we are living in the end times, and more people are turning to Yeshua as they read the New Testament.

So yes, young people are seeking – they are reading Harry Potter and exploring spirituality, watching TV and films. All this can be bad in one sense, but on the other hand it means their minds are open and, when offered, they are willing to read the New Testament. A few years ago they would have been afraid to take a New Testament when offered – not now! Today they will take a copy and read it and realize it is a very Jewish book and quite different to what they thought. I hear them say, "It's very different to what I thought or had been told." They see the world is against us Jews and they are trying to understand the times in which we live and the meaning of their lives. So when we go out on the streets and give away Bibles and share our testimonies, people are keen to listen.

We went up to Haifa recently and gave away hundreds of Bibles in Hebrew, Arabic, and Russian to people on the streets. People were happy to take a copy, and as a result we are receiving a lot of enquiries from people, particularly via the internet. Many young people here spend a lot of time on their computers, and today there are many Messianic websites for them to discover where they can find answers to their questions. Social media is widely used here in Israel and is a great tool for being in touch with people. I see more and more openness. We see the potential for a large harvest, but we need labourers to bring in the harvest and mentor and teach these new believers. As the Messianic community here grows in strength and confidence, I believe we will increasingly be noticed and be that light to the world.

The prophet Zechariah wrote,

"In those days ten men from all languages and nations will take firm hold of one Jew by the hem of his robe and say, 'Let us go with you, because we have heard that God is with you.'"[74]

I tell our young people to get ready for that day!

CHAPTER 11

Mazen Naswari – a Palestinian Pastor in the Old City of Jerusalem

It's March 2011. Come with me to the Old City of Jerusalem. After walking through the Christian Quarter from the Jaffa Gate, we turn right and then left and enter a narrow street to find the door of the Evangelical Alliance Church. The heavy metal door is kept locked. We ring the bell, a voice is heard speaking to us through the intercom, and a buzzer sounds as the door is unlocked and we enter a hallway. Stepping inside, we climb the stairs to find ourselves in a large meeting room – this is where the people gather every Sunday and where many activities take place during the week. The people who attend this church are all Palestinians who live close to the church; evangelical Christians living as a minority among a majority Muslim Palestinian population.

The issue of identity is very strong in Israel and the Middle East. Everybody is labelled. If you are not Jewish then you must be Christian or Muslim. The majority of

Christians align themselves to the Orthodox churches, including Greek, Syrian, Catholic, or Coptic churches. Jews can be from a religious Orthodox, traditional, or secular background. Arabs can be Israeli Arabs (those living within Israel) or Palestinians (those living in the West Bank or Gaza Strip), although many Israeli Arabs describe themselves as Palestinians in order to identify with those living elsewhere. Israeli Arabs are either Muslim or Christian (mainly Orthodox but with an increasing number of evangelicals), while the Palestinian population is overwhelmingly Muslim.

As Mazen's story reveals, he had a traditional Christian Orthodox background which meant he went to church two or three times a year at Christmastime, Eastertime, and perhaps for a wedding or baptism. He would be the first to admit that he had no personal belief or faith; he was simply following religious traditions.

But, at the Alliance Church, there is life! As this story reveals, the evangelical Christians living in the Old City of Jerusalem are a vibrant and envisioned group of people. I was there to meet Mazen Naswari, the pastor.

When I arrived, he was busy preparing a Bible study for a group of Palestinian young men who had recently become Christians. They had, he told me, come from a background of violence, drug abuse, and disillusionment. And Mazen understands how difficult it is for these young men, because that is part of his story. So how did he move from being a gambler and involved in drugs to being a Christian pastor?

I was born close to this church in the Old City of Jerusalem, but I was twenty-nine years old before I came to know the Lord. I am sad it took me so long to find Him.

Throughout my childhood I lived in a climate of tension and trouble between Palestinians and the Jewish people. When I was eighteen the trouble escalated once again, and during the intifada which started in 1989 and lasted until 1993, I was so unhappy with the political situation in this country that I decided to leave Jerusalem. Leaving my parents and the rest of the family behind, I went south to Eilat and lived there for seven years. But those were the worst years of my life. I quickly fell into bad company; I went to parties and ended up addicted to gambling. My life spiralled downwards. I saw many things. I learned many things, most of them bad. However, in hindsight, while I regret so much of what happened during those years, I can now see how the Lord is using that experience for good.

When I was twenty-seven my father became very ill so I returned to Jerusalem. At first, I continued doing the things I had been doing in Eilat – playing cards, gambling, and drinking. But God started working in my life as soon as I returned here. He started moving in my heart and I decided that I wanted to make a fresh start in my life. I was tired of the way I had been living, but I didn't know what to do to escape from my lifestyle that had become so addictive.

One day in 1999 I was walking through the Old City; it was Eastertime. My attention was drawn to some live music being performed by a group of young people (I later found out they were from the Alliance Church). As I listened, I realized they were singing about Jesus, and it really touched my heart.

Now I am a musician – a drummer – so the sound of music always attracts my attention, and so I tentatively opened the door of the church and went inside. I had played with many music bands in the past, but as I watched those young people worshipping the Lord, my heart was strangely moved because those people were not good musicians, but they had a really special spirit. I loved it.

When the band finished playing, a man got up to speak. I could have left then, but for some reason I stayed. Perhaps it was the worship music that had spoken so deeply to my troubled heart because as he talked about Jesus and as I listened intently to him, I knew the Lord was calling me; I could hear His voice: "Come to me." So I decided there and then to open my heart to the Lord and to follow Him.

As soon as I left the church that night and went back out into the narrow streets of the Old City thinking about all that had just happened, I saw a group of my friends. They were sitting and drinking alcohol. They invited me to go and sit with them, but I told them that I didn't want to. But they persuaded me to join them and so, reluctantly, I sat down with them. That proved to be a disastrous night for me. We went to a pub and ended up having an ugly fight with a group of other guys. I don't know how I managed to reach my home that night.

The next day I felt distraught. How could I have done such a foolish thing? Angry at myself for being so easily led astray, I was now more determined than ever to leave my old life behind. I wanted to be free from the things I had been doing; that lifestyle no longer held any attraction for me. In fact, I wanted to get as far away from it as possible and start a new page of my life by following Jesus.

For the next three months I searched for answers to the many questions that were in my mind. Is God real? Is there really eternal life? Was the message I heard at that meeting real? I started to read a Bible and gradually unexpected things started to happen. Various people came across my path; I realize now they were divine appointments. I remember two guys in particular. They were living in my apartment and they were Christians. They started talking to me about Jesus. At that time I had a shop in the Old City, and my neighbour started talking to me about Jesus!

There were many other people I met during those three months, and they all talked to me about Jesus! I was amazed because I quickly realized that this was no coincidence; rather, God was sending these people to talk to me about Him. My cousin, who hadn't been a believer up to this point, started holding a Bible study in his house. He called me and invited me to join his group. I agreed and went there for many weeks. I had never read the Bible before and I was curious to find out what it was all about. I had been brought up in an Orthodox Christian family and been to church on occasions, but I had never read the Bible before. I was very hungry to know what was written in the Word of God.

Three months later, a friend of mine (a blind person and drug addict), who had lived with me during my time in Eilat, lost his mother; she passed away. So I went to his house to visit him and while there, much to my surprise, he asked if I would accompany him to the church. I knew him well and found it hard to believe that he had started going to church because he had been such a hardened drug user, and as a result had lost his sight. And here he was asking me to take him to the church the following day! Reluctantly, I agreed.

When I arrived the following evening, I told him that I would walk with him to the church, leave him there and collect him an hour later to bring him home. But he insisted that I stay in the church with him. We argued. I told him that I had been at work all day and was very hungry and needed something to eat. But he was adamant and told me that I must stay with him in the church. As I listened to him, I heard the same voice that I had heard that Eastertime when I had heard singing coming from the building as I was walking past. The Lord was saying to me, "Come to me." So I went up the stairs to the church with my blind friend, and during the meeting that night I had the same experience as before. Now I was sure the Lord was talking to me.

I told Him that I had wanted to commit myself to Him before but I had failed and fallen back into my old way of life. I told Him that I wanted to commit myself to Him again, and I asked Him to make sure that this time I would not fail. It was as though the curtains on my eyes had been drawn back; I saw things in a different way. I saw God in a different way, I saw the Bible in a different way, and the next day I realized I was a totally different person. My life had changed. I knew that I was a new person, and I have followed Him from that day until now!

I no longer had any desire for gambling, smoking, drinking, or women: I was a different person. Externally nothing had changed: I was still living within a political situation that I found frustrating. However, I discovered that when someone comes to the Lord, new things enter their life. These are the fruits of the Holy Spirit, and include forgiveness. I had done some very bad things in my life. And I knew God had forgiven me.

My heart was full of love and so I was able to love people who didn't like me. As a Palestinian living in Israel, I was living alongside Jewish people who didn't like me or the people group I belonged to. Today, because I know Jesus Christ and understand how much God loves me, I am able to love anybody, whether they are Muslim or Jewish people! God has changed the attitudes in my heart and filled me with His compassion and love for people, whoever they are. I meet with many Jewish pastors and we are building strong relationships and praying together. We know that in our unity, God is moving and changing the spiritual atmosphere and people are coming to know Jesus. This is our unity: we have different opinions when it comes to politics, but we know we are brothers in Jesus Christ and we can sit together and pray together, despite our differences.

This movement is growing. God is moving in miraculous ways. I will share with you some stories of what God is doing here in Jerusalem at this time. Last week we had a meeting in the church and a Muslim man came to the church; we share the love of Christ with everybody. He came up the stairs to our meeting room and he told us he was unwell. One of our guys started sharing with him about how Jesus Christ used to heal people and how Jesus loves him. He asked him if he would like Jesus to heal him. And he said, "Yes, I want to get healed." He was tired of being unwell for so long.

So our guy told him, "OK, we'll pray together." And the Muslim man prayed that Jesus would touch his life and heal him.

We share the love of Christ with everybody here – Jews, Muslims, even [Orthodox] Christians. We believe there are two kingdoms: the kingdom of hell and the kingdom of heaven. It doesn't matter whether people are Jews or Muslims or Christians; if they have a relationship with Jesus, they will be accepted into the kingdom of heaven and they will go into eternal life to be with God eternally. Unless they accept Jesus, they will not go to heaven when they die. We share this message with everyone who is willing to listen. This is our faith and the truth that we believe in.

If that sounds bold and courageous, it is because it is the truth that has changed me. Jesus has changed my life. My life was in darkness. Knowing Jesus has brought meaning into my life so I know He can bring meaning to others. Many people here live in darkness and emptiness. Many of the young people living in this neighbourhood don't know what to do with their lives. Many families are broken. I know that believing in Jesus is the solution. So if I don't share this with the people I meet, I will be selfish. I share the message about Jesus because He has changed my life and given meaning – I cannot hide it.

When I became a Christian at the age of twenty-nine I asked the Lord why it had taken so long. I was sad that I had wasted so many years of my life. While I was considering this question, I was looking around and saw many others, many of them friends, who didn't know Him. So I decided to share my testimony with the people I knew, people who could remember what I had been like in the past. Gradually I found myself also wanting to share my testimony with other people, folk I didn't know. I wanted them to hear about the change that knowing and believing in Jesus had made in my life. What had started as a prayer in my heart, "Lord, use me in your kingdom," became a reality as I told more and more people my story.

By the year 2000 my wife and I (we were newly married) started praying together, "Lord, use us." Very quickly the Lord opened a door for me to work in a Christian organization giving out Bibles and Christian films to anybody who was interested. I was sitting with people and sharing with them about the love of Christ, and the leaders of the church saw that I was keen to be very active in the ministry. As a result, they invited me to come and join the team of workers in the church. My wife and I prayed and we agreed that this was something I should do. So I joined the team here as an intern. I didn't know much at that time and so I started to study the Bible and gain some Christian education. In 2008 I was invited to become the co-pastor of the church, and in 2010 I became the pastor.

Today, people from many backgrounds come here. We are situated in a Palestinian area of the Old City where both Christian people and Muslim people live, and our doors are open to anybody. We are here for those who want to come and pray. People are meeting God here. We don't close the door to anybody. The majority of people who come here are Christian people, but increasingly we are welcoming Muslims who are really interested. They know Jesus as a healer. They know Jesus as someone important. Some know Him as a prophet. But they come and find they feel comfortable here. I am not saying that they are Christians, but they feel God's comfort here; they sense a good spirit and so they come.

The majority of people coming to our church are young people. We have meetings for older women, meetings for young women, meetings for the youth, meetings for young couples, and meetings for the children. The young people are very active and love the Lord and are keen to help us in running the ministry here.

While we are busy seeing this evangelical church growing in the Old City, at the same time we are in touch with Messianic Jewish congregations in Jerusalem, and their numbers too are growing. I can see that God is moving here in Israel and the West Bank at this time.

I would say again, the love of God is for everyone. He loves the Jews, He loves the Christians, and He loves the Arabs and Palestinians. God is moving among us all. I believe that Jesus is coming soon. Something is happening. Many people are coming back to knowing Him as their Saviour and I feel that the love of the Lord is everywhere, including between Arab and Jewish believers. This shows that God is moving. All of us who believe in Jesus are members of one family.

I, along with other Arab/Palestinian pastors, meet regularly with Jewish pastors here in Jerusalem. I consider them as brothers of mine. Jesus Himself said when praying for His disciples:

> "My prayer is not for them alone. I pray also for those who will believe in me through their message, that all of them may be one, Father, just as you are in me and I am in you. May they also be in us so that the world may believe that you have sent me."[75]

We can love each other even if we have different opinions on other matters. In this way we show the world that Jesus is alive. This is something the politicians cannot do. This love that we as believers in Jesus share, no matter what background we come from, shows that we can love one another.

We all, Jewish believers and Arab/Palestinian Christians, realize that this is a situation that has never happened before, and yes, I can see that it is growing; it is as though we have reached a new stage in the spiritual kingdom of Jesus Christ. When I came to the church in 1999 we had sixty people in the church. We met in a small room and things were hardly moving. Now we have three churches with 250 members! In this church we have 120 people. We have four ministries that work from here. So God is moving! This is something really new.

I also meet regularly on a monthly basis with Arab pastors in Jerusalem. We share our news and pray for each other. And because this church is located in Jerusalem, this is an ideal place where both Arab and Jewish pastors can come and meet and pray together. We share news of what God is doing in our churches and congregations. It's important. It's important for the world around to see that Arabs and Jews can be together. We don't solve all the conflicts. We recognize that we come from different backgrounds and different nations, and we are well aware of the history of all the conflicts that we experience in this region. But, despite all, we know that we share the love of Jesus and we pray for each other and for each other's hurts, and we pray that our nation will come to Christ. I believe that only through Jesus can there be a political solution in this land. This is why it is so important that we meet together.

Being a musician, I have a particular interest in worship music and developing our worship team of singers and musicians. We often visit other churches – sometimes Palestinian churches in the West Bank, sometimes other Arab churches in Jerusalem or the north of the country, and sometimes Messianic Jewish congregations. Tomorrow there is a conference in Eilat where we are expecting 150 young people – Arabs and Jews from various churches and congregations throughout the country – to come to worship God together. Our music group will be singing in Arabic; there will also be a worship group singing in Hebrew. I came to know Jesus through hearing worship music, so to have such an event with Arab and Jewish young people worshipping God together is, I believe, going to have a profound effect on their young lives. It is my prayer that they will not see each other as enemies, but as a close family, brothers and sisters with one Father, united in Jesus. It is good for Arab and Jewish young believers to get together to talk and pray for our country. It will help to change the mentality and the idea that we cannot live together. Instead it will prove that we can talk together and be friends.

We are encouraged that we are located in this area of the Old City, just around the corner from the Christian Quarter and on the edge of the Muslim Quarter, and only a short walk from the Church of the Holy Sepulchre. I can't say I've always thought this way about living here, especially when I was a teenager, owing to the political situation. But when I eventually came to faith at the age of twenty-nine and started reading the Bible, I realized how this city of Jerusalem is so special on the heart of God that now I am really so proud to live here in this country and to serve the church and to serve the people here in the land.

We mainly work with Arab people, with Christians in the church, but in the wider community we are increasingly involved in social work among people from both Christian backgrounds and Muslim backgrounds. We are showing the love of the Lord through different activities, most recently (with the help of friends in an organization we work closely with) by giving food packages to needy people. We see how they smile when they receive this help. Sometimes they want to know why we do this, and we share that it is through the love that Jesus has put in our heart. There is a lot of poverty, especially on the Arab side. In some houses around here we find many people living together in overcrowded conditions and they are hardly able to meet their monthly needs. Inevitably, both parents are working, and at the end of the month they are scarcely able to manage.

I believe that Jesus is coming back soon. The Bible has much to say about the last days. Many people are coming to salvation throughout many places in the world. Healings are happening. Spiritual gifts are evident. People are expectant. All these things make me believe His return is soon.

I would particularly like Christians in the West to see that God is moving in the Arab nations of the world. The Middle East area is hidden from many eyes and I have noticed that Christians from the West are ignorant about the fact that there are Arab believers in Jesus. When I have the opportunity to speak and I share with them and tell them that I am from Israel, they think I must be Jewish. When they hear that I am a Palestinian believer they are shocked. God loves even the Arabs and the Palestinians. Many people may think badly about the Palestinians, but God loves them and He loves the Arab nations and wants them to come to salvation.

I would like to share this message with the church in the West: please pray for us. We are living with very hard circumstances. Currently in the nations of the Middle East there are many wars. People in Egypt, Lebanon, Syria, and beyond are suffering from the effects of political upheaval and the resultant wars that are ongoing. But God loves them, and I would like to encourage Christians in the West to pray for these people, that God will comfort them and bring them to salvation.

We see God moving in unexpected ways. Two years ago a young man, who is a television producer, came to talk to us because he wanted to make a programme about what life is like for Palestinian teenagers living in Jerusalem and the West Bank. He was not a believer in Jesus but he wanted to use our location here in the Old City. I asked the elders and they agreed. Six months ago he moved to live in an area on the outskirts of Bethlehem within the West Bank, and he invited us to visit him. We went and shared with him about Jesus. Then he invited us to visit a friend of his. So again, we went. From then on, we were invited to many houses where we sat and prayed with many people. Then he asked us to arrange a regular meeting for these people in the area. We readily agreed and told him that if he invited people, we would go and share with them. Thirty young people and a few elderly people started to meet, and today we go there every week and teach them from the Bible. All of them have accepted the Lord.

It is so encouraging to see how God has blessed something that had such small beginnings and that now God has opened a new church in a different location with a different kind of people. As we recognize and embrace these small opportunities, we see God opening doors of opportunity that constantly surprise and delight us.

CHAPTER 12

Patrick Radecker – an Outcast from Society Finds Faith in Yeshua

When I first met Patrick in May 2010 he looked extremely ill. He had just arrived at Beit Nitzachon (House of Victory), a faith-based drug and alcohol rehab centre in Haifa, northern Israel, where the director, Eric Benson, is a Christian from the United States. The philosophy of Beit Nitzachon is very simple – prayer. And it works, because when I saw Patrick sixteen months later I didn't recognize him. He had transformed from a man who had been at death's door to a man who looked fit, bright, and happy.

Since then, I have met Patrick on a number of occasions and each time noticed a further change in him physically, mentally, and spiritually.

In March 2015 I interviewed Patrick again. We met in Haifa where he is working as a chef in a Messianic Jewish guest house. He served us coffee and a delicious assortment of cakes and biscuits that he had made. Here is a man who, despite losing so many years of his life to drugs and alcohol, has found a reason to live again. His story is quite simply of a man who has been snatched from the jaws of death and given another chance at life, a chance he has seized with all his heart.

So who is Patrick, and why is his story included in this book? Like so many people I have interviewed in Israel and the West Bank over the past twenty years, his story is one example of what God is doing in the land today in taking people who find themselves on the margins of society – outside the camp, so to speak – and restoring and rebuilding their lives and placing them back in the situations from which they came in order to bring others to know Him. That so many people living in Israel, both Arabs and Jews, struggle with addiction to drugs and alcohol is perhaps evidence of a spiritual battle that is going on for the heart and soul of this nation. That so many have been rescued and brought "back to life" to pursue and fulfil their God-given destiny is perhaps further evidence that ultimately God can rescue any life – nobody is too far from His reach if they are willing to respond and take hold of His hand.

Here we explore Patrick's story and, in placing it alongside the others in this book, we see the larger picture of what God is doing in Israel today.

I was born in 1967 in Holland into a Jewish family. When I was very young my parents decided to move to Australia, and when I was nine years old they moved again; this time to Israel. I hated living in Israel. By the age of thirteen I was smoking, using soft drugs, and drinking alcohol. When I was fourteen and a half years old, my parents threw me out of the house because my behaviour had become so erratic. I gave my parents a lot of grief because I did not want to live here; it was the only way I knew of rebelling against them, and I didn't care what I was doing to them or myself because I hated being alive. By the age of seventeen I was using hard drugs, and for the next twenty-four years I was a heroin addict.

I juggled my way through life, and for a time managed to stay one step ahead of disaster. I became a sous chef even while being dependent on heroin. Here I was second-in-command to the head chef, overseeing the preparation and cooking of food in high-class restaurants. It was a responsible position and for a time I managed to hide my addiction. While I was working and earning a good wage, feeding my drug habit was not too difficult.

But eventually I no longer had the desire, or ability, to work. I could not cope with reality any more. I just wanted to use as many drugs as I could, as often as I could. I was no longer able to afford the rent to live in a house so I moved out, and for seven years I lived on the streets. Latterly I was using three to four grams of heroin at a time and injecting every day as well as drinking a litre to a litre and a half of alcohol every day. I was popping as many tablets as I could. And on top of that I was smoking crack, although I didn't really like it. If I had a good day and had enough money, smoking some crack was like a dessert after a meal.

That was my life and I didn't know how I would escape from it. I was begging for money in the daytime, and at night I was collecting bottles to sell; that is how I got the money to buy drugs.

I tried twenty-five to thirty secular rehabilitation centres, but none of them could help me, and I thought I would never be off drugs. The people who knew me from all the rehab places where I had been throughout Israel, when they saw me begging for money in Tel Aviv would say, "Oh Patrick, we're really sorry but we don't have room for you any more."

I would encourage them by saying, "Well, I know I'm bad for statistics. It's OK, you don't have to say you're sorry. I know I'm bad."

And that was that. I gave up hoping that I would ever recover. That was until one day when I met a man called Rod Powell. Rod and his wife are both from America and had been missionaries in Russia for many years before moving to Israel. Rod approached me on the streets where I was living in Tel Aviv and gradually we became friends. One day he gave me a Bible. I read some verses and a sentence stuck in my mind:

> "You did not choose me, but I chose you to go and bear fruit – fruit that will last."[76]

I did not know who "me" was. I had heard about Jesus, but I could not make the connection to Him because the picture I had of Jesus in my mind was of a blue-eyed, blond-haired, beautiful, Swedish-nosed Jesus. When people told me he was from Bethlehem and grew up in Nazareth, I just could not believe they were talking about the same person. I thought he was a Swedish god who was born here in Israel and they took him back to Sweden and now some people wanted to bring him back to Israel again; I thought it was a hoax. But on the other hand, I wanted to try to find out the truth and whether or not He was real, because I did not want to continue living on the streets with this habit that I had. I knew it was not good for me and was gradually destroying me, yet somehow I was convinced I was not going to die from taking drugs; I had a glimmer of hope that at some point in my life I would recover.

Three months after being given the Bible, a place became available for me at the House of Victory, and that was a blessing. However, to begin with I thought I had lost my mind because I couldn't remember anything. I was reading and reading and reading but I could not remember what I was reading about. I thought something was wrong with me. I asked Eric Benson, the director of House of Victory, "What's wrong with me?" and he told me to just continue!

"Persevere, Patrick."

Persevere? I didn't even know that word!

So I continued, and one day I found in the Gospel of John a verse that changed my life, because there I read:

"I am the vine; you are the branches. If a man remains in me and I in him, he will bear much fruit; apart from me you can do nothing."[77]

I needed to hear that because up until then I had no prayer life and I was at a crossroads. All I knew was I didn't want to go back on to the streets. If God was not going to show me now what to do, I was going to leave the House of Victory because I was fed up. I got down on my knees and said, "God, if You chose me, You've got to change me because I know You don't like me like this."

That prayer changed my life. I thank God for Eric Benson for putting up with a problematic person like me.

By the time I was forty-three years old I had been free from drugs for sixteen months, the first time in my adult life. I cannot describe the freedom I felt. Even when I was working as a chef, although I was happy at work, I was never free. There was never a light at the end of the tunnel. Today, I love telling my friends on the streets that there is hope and there is freedom, that those who Jesus sets free are "free indeed".[78]

Can I be sure that I will not slip back into drugs again? I am sure that I am not going to go back on drugs because first of all I have Jesus and my strength is that I am His. I ask Him specifically not to let me ever put a needle in my vein or a straw in my mouth or up my nose again. I used to pray this prayer every day, several times a day, but now I know He knows my heart and He has burned on my heart a freedom. I am free, and I want to proclaim this freedom to everybody who hasn't received it yet. I know that God has called me to evangelize and proclaim this freedom.

When people who knew me before see me now, they can hardly believe what they see. I can hardly believe what I see when I look in the mirror in the morning! I know Jesus is not going to let go of me.

For forty-two years I did whatever I wanted, and from now on I just want to do what He wants me to do. I could have died so many times. Now I know Jesus and know He has rescued me from my past and given me a sense of destiny; pursuing that destiny is the only thing that matters to me now.

I would also like the nations around Israel to know our God. As Jeremiah said, we are a "stiff-necked" people,[79] yet God has a plan for us, not because of anything we do but because we have a great God.

I can hardly believe that today I am married and working with a Messianic community here in northern Israel that embraces Jews and Arabs and people from the nations. I am an evangelist and spend as much time as I have available going back on to the streets to talk to people who are drug addicts and share my story of deliverance with them.

But I can well remember the day I was due to move on from the House of Victory and start to stand on my own two feet again. I was very afraid and always thought people were looking at me. Having been so long on drugs and now being clean, there is an effective paranoia the enemy brings to make you afraid of everything that moves. By the grace of God, I had Rod and Margee Powell who helped me with many things. They were like a buffer-zone ministry and were very important to me at this time because the enemy just does not want us to be clean; he wants to keep us on the streets, more dead than alive. So for almost two years Margee would do all my payments of bills because I was too embarrassed to walk into the bank. I would give her the money (I was accountable to them as well, which was very good for me) and she would help me in this way. I knew that although I was a believer in Yeshua and He had freed me from years of being addicted to drugs and alcohol, I had to be careful as I was a new believer and still vulnerable.

I think it's very clear where in 1 Peter it's written,

> Be self-controlled and alert. Your enemy the
> devil prowls around like a roaring lion looking for
> someone to devour.[80]

For me, to be accountable was important. I have made mistakes and I have fallen. But, thank God, each time I fall I come back to the foot of the cross and repent, and the Lord is forgiving; He wants to give us life.

It took me a couple of years to really start standing on my own two feet. After that time I had the courage to go into the bank to open an account. I used to receive my salary by cheque each month from the congregation and would immediately go and cash it. But one day I decided I would go to the bank myself and open an account. I went in and it all went so smoothly! I had always been afraid that they would look down their noses at me and say, "Where were you for those seven years that you didn't have a bank account?" The enemy uses these things to make us feel ashamed, and we shouldn't be. Now I have even ordered a credit card! After living for all those years on the streets and losing everything, now I am slowly coming back into society.

I met Sharon, my wife, about three years ago. Unbeknown to me, the Lord had told her that I would be her husband. I liked her. But I never really wanted to get married, because of my childhood experience of being physically abused by my father; I was afraid that I would physically abuse. So it took me quite a while to decide that I wanted to marry Sharon, and it was only when the Lord showed me from the Scriptures that Sharon was the best thing He had for me that I proposed to her. She had been coming to Israel for twenty years and was often in our congregation.

Sharon is not Jewish. She has been a Christian for more than thirty years so we have very different backgrounds. This was one of the questions in my mind when considering whether I could marry her. How could I be the spiritual head of the house when in comparison I was relatively new to the faith? It was the Holy Spirit who reassured me that it wasn't about the number of years somebody had been a believer that mattered, so when I realized this, I popped the question!

Sharon and I were married on 8 October 2014. Holding my chuppah[81] were four of my friends. Two were Jewish – one a Sabrah, or native–born Israeli, and one Russian Jewish immigrant. The third was a Gentile Christian friend, and the fourth was an Arab Christian friend from Ramallah. This was particularly symbolic for us as it represented the "one new man" referred to in Ephesians:

> For he himself is our peace, who has made the two
> one and has destroyed the barrier, the dividing wall
> of hostility, by abolishing in his flesh the law with
> its commandments and regulations. His purpose
> was to create in himself one new man out of the
> two, thus making peace, and in this one body to
> reconcile both of them to God through the cross,
> by which he put to death their hostility.[82]

I really believe that God has rescued my life for a purpose, and part of my destiny is linked to what God is doing here in Israel in these days. I love evangelizing and talking to people about Yeshua, even in the supermarket. It's an amazing privilege that God has given me.

A documentary filmmaker made a programme about me when I was living on the streets, and when secular people see it, it touches their hearts. I find there is great openness towards Messianic believers today in Israel. When I share my story with ordinary people, they are touched and interested and want to know more.

I go to Tel Aviv in the daytime to an area called the Last Stop, a derelict area in Tel Aviv where the old bus station used to be. It's a desperate place and as I walk around talking to the hundreds of addicts and prostitutes who live there – men and girls – I often see people I know. When they see me they often cry because they don't always recognize me at first now that I am looking so well.

I remember one girl I met – she was so shocked to see me that she wouldn't let me go until I gave her a book. She wanted to know where I had been to recover and begged me to take her there. Addicts who are women are often prostitutes, so helping them is doubly difficult; they are extremely wounded people both emotionally and physically. But the House of Victory only takes in men; there is a great need for similar houses for girls. She wouldn't let go of me; she was so amazed to see me alive and to hear my story. "Tell me what happened to you," she kept saying. We tell them that there is a Saviour, and I tell them that unless they accept Yeshua and ask for His help, they will die, and judgment awaits us all.

We have an awesome God, and He brought about my transformation. Sometimes when I talk to people they find it very hard to believe that just five years earlier I was living on the streets just like they are, and I was in an even worse condition than they are. Because it's a supernatural transformation it doesn't take ten or fifteen years to recover: our God can change somebody's situation in a second if He so wants. My recovery is entirely supernatural. It has come about through believing that Yeshua is my Saviour and by studying the Word of God. We have to learn to hold on to promises. In Joel it is written:

> "I will repay you for the years the locusts have eaten."[83]

When somebody finds it hard to believe that I was once in their state, I show them a clip of the documentary film that was made about my life, showing me as I was then, scouring rubbish bins for empty bottles, drinking the dregs, and selling the bottles for a few shekels. I say all this humbly because it's not my work; it's the work of the Lord. God doesn't need me but He can use me, and I count it an amazing privilege to go out there and reach out to these men and women.

After forty-three years of living in darkness and despair, sometimes I am asked if I have any regrets about all the years I lost. My answer is to say that I know our God is sovereign. He allows us to go through difficult situations; some people call them tests. In my case, it wasn't God who took me into years of drug addiction; rather the enemy who wanted to destroy my life and keep me in bondage to the overwhelming power of that addiction. However, God had His hand upon me all the time and He didn't let me die. I experienced at least eight overdoses and was in hospital numerous times. But one day God said, "This guy that's shooting in his thigh and in his neck, I'm going to use him. I'm going to take him out – he's ripe now." I wouldn't be the person I am today, with the compassion I have for those people who are still in the place where I have come from, if I hadn't gone through it. So somebody who works in Wall Street and one day is saved has compassion for the man sitting next to him who is also a lawyer and totally absorbed by that lifestyle. I wouldn't understand that. God uses everybody in different ways. He wants everybody to be saved, not only the junkies!

I am now part of a community of believers, many of whom have similar stories to myself and have been through difficult life experiences. I used to hate living in Israel. But now I am happy to say I am Jewish and live here. I am excited as I look at the bigger picture of what God is doing here in Israel and the wider Middle East today, and meet with others who also have a strong sense of destiny.

Recently God has given me a greater heart for the Arab nations. I attended a reconciliation conference in northern Cyprus for both Jewish believers and Arab Christians, which was life-changing. Every Jewish and Arab believer should go to one of these conferences to see the amazing transformation that God is doing in giving both people groups the heart to pray for the other. My wife and I do pray for the Arab nations around us, that we can work and pray together as we all try to better understand the biblical role of Israel in God's purposes.

While at the conference, I asked God to show me something small to help me understand my role in His purposes. With so much trouble swirling around us in the Middle East, it is sometimes hard to see what we as individuals can do. He is very specific, and when I arrived at the conference I heard the testimonies of many people, including two Egyptian sisters. I found myself crying tears of repentance when I heard how they had come to faith through reading Romans chapter 11. It was so precious to hear them praying for Israel and us praying for them, not only for the Christians, but for the Muslims too, that they would be saved. There are already many Arab people from the nations surrounding Israel coming to faith in Yeshua – we want to see a tidal wave! I had heard so many stories, but hearing stories and actually meeting the people concerned is a totally different thing. I know the

Bible says, "Blessed are those who believe and don't see," but seeing and believing is doubly life-changing!

Today we are living in times when we are seeing Bible prophecy unfolding. Zechariah 12:2–3 is happening now:

> "I am going to make Jerusalem a cup that sends all the surrounding peoples reeling … On that day, when all the nations of the earth are gathered against her, I will make Jerusalem an immovable rock for all the nations. All who try to move it will injure themselves."

Jerusalem is a very big stumbling block for the world. We are encouraged, however, because in that same chapter of Zechariah we read:

> "And I will pour out on the house of David and the inhabitants of Jerusalem a spirit of grace and supplication. They will look on me, the one they have pierced, and they will mourn for him as one mourns for an only child, and grieve bitterly for him as one grieves for a firstborn son."[84]

We are waiting expectantly for that day, and we believe it is just around the corner.

I've given up on making plans. Every day I say, "Lord, here I am." We are all trying to hear His voice encouraging us as to what to do each day. I wouldn't mind at all if God told me to go to any nation – I would go without hesitation. For now, I believe I am called here to the people of Israel, whether it's in the supermarkets, on the bus, or at the Last Stop in Tel Aviv. It's an amazing privilege.

The Story of The Olive Tree Reconciliation Fund

The people you have met through reading the stories in this book have, I hope, given you an insight into how God is working in Israel and the wider Middle East through the lives of individual people. I also hope that now you have read these stories you will have not only a greater desire to pray for these people, but also a desire to be involved in practical ways. As I mentioned in the introduction, the most important question that The Olive Tree programme asks is, "What is God doing in Israel and the wider Middle East today?"

So if, having read the stories in this book, you are now feeling that you would like to help in some way, let me tell you the story of The Olive Tree Reconciliation Fund (OTRF). I could never have imagined starting a charity, but that is what happened in 2008 as a direct result of people sending gifts of money to pass on to the Jewish and Arab believers living in Israel and the Palestinian areas that they had been reading about in books or articles I had written, or in radio programmes they had heard.

In the beginning

It all started with an article about the plight of Arab Christians in Bethlehem – in particular, those belonging to the evangelical community there. For those of you who are passionate about supporting Israel, this article posed a challenge: can we feed first and talk theology afterwards? I wrote then:

> **I am not saying that theology does not matter.**
> **Of course it does. Those who disagree with**
> **Replacement theology (as I most certainly do)**
> **will never change the situation in Bethlehem**
> **by taking a stand-offish attitude. We have to go**
> **there, whether in prayer or in person, and get**
> **our hands dirty and help the people – otherwise**
> **there will soon be no Christian Arabs left in**
> **Bethlehem.**

The article went on to describe the heartache experienced by one evangelical pastor in particular, and the sacrificial way in which he helped the people there, both Christians and Muslims.

The response to that article was overwhelming – and every penny donated was sent to the pastor in Bethlehem for him to give to those in need. It demonstrated that Christians in the UK, who love Israel and the Jewish people, also love and support the Arab Christians and recognize the work of reconciliation that is going on between Arab Christians and Messianic Jewish believers in the Holy Land today.

Muslim Arabs have to taste Jesus; Jewish people have to see Him

In previous books I have written about Labib Madanat, Middle East Director of Bible Society ministry. From a Jordanian family, he works with Arab and Jewish believers as they take the gospel to both religious and secular Jews, as well as to Muslim Palestinians. I wrote, "Labib knows from years of experience that true love and concern is primarily practical. 'Muslim Arabs have to taste Jesus,' he told me, 'Jewish people have to see Him.'"

In various articles I shared a couple of projects, ways in which Christians in the nations could support Labib Madanat and his teams, including those working in Gaza. And once again, people gave generously. So when news broke about the murder of Rami Ayyad in October 2007, hearts were open and the plight of his young widow, Pauline (who was expecting their third child), and their two young children prompted another flush of generosity.

Rami was the manager of the Bible Society bookshop in Gaza city. He was kidnapped one Saturday afternoon in October 2007 as he was closing the shop. Concerned he was late home, Pauline described how she had called her husband on his mobile phone. Rami replied to say he had been "delayed" and may be late. Pauline realized something was wrong and called Rami's brother, who also called Rami on his mobile phone. Rami replied and managed to tell his brother that he was being held by a group and would be "away for a long time". After that the phone was switched off. Rami's body was found the next morning. He had been tortured before being murdered and his body dumped.

The response to Rami's death, especially by Messianic Jewish believers living in Israel, was unprecedented. A special fund was established to support Pauline and her three children (she gave birth to a baby daughter shortly after Rami's death). The pain remains. Rami did not die in vain. But the needs are ongoing.

Persecution

As you will have read in the opening chapters of this book, in March 2008 Ami Ortiz, the teenage son of Messianic pastors David and Leah Ortiz, was cruelly injured when he opened what looked like a gift of food kindly left on the doorstep of the family's apartment in Ariel, Samaria. But it wasn't a gift; it was a bomb that blew up in Ami's face and almost killed him. Ami's recovery has been slow and painful. His medical bills have been huge. Once again, readers responded generously and today Ami has made a miraculous recovery.

Helping the stranger

During 2008 I wrote about the plight of Sudanese refugees in Israel and how one Messianic Jewish believer found herself providing a refuge for these beleaguered people. Today, the question of helping the large numbers of African refugees pouring into Israel has become a national issue. I was told by somebody who was helping these people:

They have escaped from the devastation of the twenty-year war perpetrated on the southern Sudanese people by the radical Islamic government in Khartoum, and the current genocide taking place in Darfur. Most had sought refuge in Egypt but found persecution and danger there as well. So, risking everything and paying hundreds of dollars to Bedouin guides, they were taken to the border with Israel and left to cross over into the desert in the dark of night. After walking for hours, Israeli soldiers would find the refugees and bring them to the base. As Sudan is an "enemy nation", they were considered a security risk and taken to prison. The army and the immigration police had no facility to care for the women and children. When I received the call, it was as if the Lord spoke a clear word to me, "This is going to be big." I had no idea that for more than a year, we would be the only place to take in Sudanese women and children. Both Muslim and Christian women from a number of different tribes in Sudan were sent to us. Many were traumatized by the events they had witnessed previously – the destruction of their village, the killing of family members, rape and imprisonment. Through persistent prayer and consistent application of God's principles, we began seeing genuine spiritual transformation in the lives of women from both Christian and Muslim backgrounds.

One new man

Andrey Teplinsky and Patrick Radecker's stories reveal the remarkable work going on at the House of Victory (Beit Nitzachon) in Haifa – a rehab centre for alcoholics and drug addicts, both Jews and Arabs. Founded by David and Karen Davis, their vision for this ministry has always been the "one new man in Messiah" (Ephesians 2:14–16). I've visited faith-based rehabilitation centres in the UK and abroad where the aim is purely to break the power of addiction. But at Beit Nitzachon they are fighting on two fronts – addiction and racial hatred – because to achieve the "one new man in Messiah" in Israel today involves demolishing the ancient wall of enmity between Jew and Arab. In today's political climate I wonder which is the greater breakthrough.

David Davis told me, "One of my greatest joys as a pastor is to witness once lost and addicted Jewish and Arabic 'sons' take their place in the body of Messiah in Israel. Graduates of House of Victory include our youth pastor, a home group leader, and media ministry leader, as well as workers at House of Victory and Beit Yedidia, our community centre. One Arab graduate is a fearless preacher of the gospel to Muslims in Jerusalem, Bethlehem, and Jericho. Only Jesus can reconcile Jews and Arabs, and He is doing it."

Reconciliation can take time

Travel with me to Netanya, a city in Israel on the Mediterranean just north of Tel Aviv. In 1974, Lisa Loden and her husband David came from America and settled there. Former hippies, both from Jewish families, they became radical believers in Jesus and came to Israel on a one-way ticket to pursue their destiny. They were some of the first Messianic believers to come to Israel for 2,000 years.

Lisa takes up the story: "When we arrived, there was no one to greet us. Here in Netanya, the city where we chose to settle, there were no other known believers at that time."

"So what is the situation there today?" I asked.

"Today the situation is vastly different to what it was when we first arrived in that both the number of believers in Messiah and the number of congregations has increased dramatically. When we arrived there were between 300 and 500 believers in the entire country; today, conservative estimates will tell you there are 10,000. When we came there was no congregation in Netanya. David and I began to meet together in our home in early 1977 in faith that God would bring others and a congregation would grow here. Today the congregation, which is called Beit Asaph, numbers more than 220."

David and Lisa have always had a passion for reconciliation. I asked Lisa where that passion came from.

"I think the early experiences you have in faith affect you very deeply, and when we came to faith, we were the 'outsider' community. My husband and I came out of the 1960s wild lifestyle so we were the outsiders in our own culture in the United States. When we came to faith we were embraced by local ordinary Christians. They loved us. They took us in. They fed us. They were so loving, and that made a tremendous impact on our lives. They didn't have to preach about unity because they lived it – they lived love. So for us it was natural and automatic that you reach out and embrace everyone."

Over the years David and Lisa have gone out of their way to meet with Arab Palestinian believers. I asked Lisa how difficult it had been.

"For me it has always been a joy. I can't say that it has been difficult. It's been painful sometimes because when you meet people and you empathize with them and you listen to their stories and you hear their struggles and their pain, it is painful. So for me it's been a challenge at times, but always a joy to be in relationship with my Arab brothers and sisters."

The question at the heart of this book has been to find out what God is doing in Israel and the West Bank today, so why does Lisa believe reconciliation between Jew and Arab is so important to Him?

"God is a healer, and He heals hearts and He heals relationships. Our whole life in faith is about our healed relationship with our creator, and this includes a healed relationship with His creation. How much more within the body of Messiah, which is the field of reconciliation in which I work, bringing together Jews and Arabs, Palestinians, and people from the nations in a common basis of faith and to live out in our daily lives what it means to be reconciled to God and to each other. God is doing an amazing thing here because wherever I look I see what I call 'flowers of hope on the dusty path of life'! You look to the side and you see there's a small bloom you didn't see before. These small blooms are relationships that are being built, friendships that are formed, commitments to each other. They are small, but they are truly hopeful. Some are growing larger all the time. I see it on a personal basis as well as in a number of congregations now. So God is doing something wonderful here, and it's the healing of an ancient breach. I think we can look back to Jacob and Esau and Isaac and Ishmael. It's a family thing for God."

"Have you been able to do this without compromising what you believe?" I asked.

"Absolutely. I think you have to come into this area of reconciliation and relationship building knowing who you are in Messiah – that's the most important thing. Our identity as believers in Him is the primary identity in our lives, and it's on that basis that we begin to build. Then we can talk about the things that divide us. They shouldn't divide us because we do have a unity for which our Messiah died."

"So what is the atmosphere like when a group of Jewish Messianic women believers meet with a group of Palestinian Christian women?"

"Well, it depends on whether it's a first meeting, or a second meeting, or a third meeting! If it's a second or a third meeting then there are hugs and kisses! Initially, women don't come to meetings like this unless something has moved in their hearts to bring them there. Sometimes there's a bit of hesitancy, primarily from the Arab sisters because the Jewish culture and mentality is probably a little more brash and outgoing than the average Arab mentality in this country. But very quickly we get through these initial walls and we see one another as women, as people. We are all either mothers or daughters. We know that we have the same basis of faith. And even with the hesitancy there is a desire and a willingness to meet together, and quite quickly we begin to form bonds of friendship."

"You must have instances when people become angry as they remember the wrongs from the past on both sides."

"Yes, that does happen, and we've learned to keep our mouths shut and listen to one another, to put our own natural defensiveness to the side to truly try to hear one another's hearts. We cannot take collective responsibility for what our peoples have done, but we can identify with the pain that our brothers and sisters suffer and be sorry for what has happened. And we have found that it goes a long way when you reach out and touch the heart of someone else, and you lay your hand on their shoulder or you take their hand in yours and you look into their eyes and in that way identify with their pain. Listening and acceptance are the keys, rather than rejection of each other."

More recently, Lisa has started teaching at The Nazareth Evangelical Theological Seminary (NETS). I asked her why she was prepared to get involved in this project.

"For so long this matter of reconciliation and relationship building between our two communities has been in my heart. And this is an opportunity to actually live it out on a weekly basis. Every week I am in Nazareth, and I am a Jewish woman teaching primarily Arab men. And it has been absolutely astounding! I am responsible for leadership development – spiritual leadership. It was very funny in the beginning and there was a lot of hesitation, but it was more because I was a woman than that I was Jewish. But I have to say that after the second lesson, God broke down all the barriers and we truly have a relationship of caring and love, and I have worked with them now for four years."

Unfolding story

And so the story of The Olive Tree Reconciliation Fund is unfolding, just as what God is doing in Israel and the surrounding nations is unfolding. It feels as though we are running to keep up with Him! Michael Kerem's account in chapter four illustrates this!

The OTRF is a registered charity (Number 1125706) which aims to build bridges of understanding and support, in a spirit of reconciliation between believers (both Jewish and Arab), in Israel and the wider Middle East with Christians worldwide. Our chief means of doing this is through gathering and thoroughly researching the stories of believers who live there before broadcasting or publishing them in order to inform Christians in the nations who are interested.

That many Christians respond to these stories by giving generously enables The OTRF to pass on every penny we receive to those in need, and the needs are great and constantly increasing.

When the focus of much of the world's media is centred on Jerusalem and what happens there in the political realm, should it not be an important area of focus for Christians to enquire as to what God is doing there today and look at the region through the lens of the Bible and the spiritual realm?

Information

For more information about The OTRF and to hear The Olive Tree radio programmes, please visit our website, www.olivetreefund.org

To receive regular news from The OTRF please email enquiries@olivetreefund.org or write to the address below. If you would like to send a gift, then please either donate online via our website or send a cheque (made out to *The Olive Tree Reconciliation Fund*) and post to OTRF, PO Box 402, Billingshurst, RH14 4BQ, UK.

Endnotes

1. **Purim parcel** The festival of **Purim** is celebrated every year on the 14th of the Hebrew month of Adar in late winter/early spring. It commemorates the salvation of the Jewish people in ancient Persia from Haman's plot to destroy, kill and annihilate all the Jews, young and old, infants and women, in a single day. The full story can be read in the book of Esther in the Old Testament. Jewish people celebrate Purim according to Mordecai's instructions as recorded in Esther 9:22: "… to observe the days as days of feasting and joy and giving presents of food to one another [mishloach manot] and gifts to the poor [mattanot la-evyonim]."

2. **Ariel** This city in central Israel was established in 1978 by forty pioneering families. Today it is home to 20,000 people comprising 18,000 residents and 10,000 students who study at the University of Ariel. Located in the heart of Israel in the hills of Samaria, it is 2,000 feet above sea level, twenty-five miles east of Tel Aviv and forty miles north of Jerusalem.

3. **The Talmud** (Hebrew for "study") is one of the central works of the Jewish people. It is the record of rabbinic teachings spanning a period of about 600 years, beginning in the first century AD and continuing through the sixth and seventh centuries AD. The rabbinic teachings of the Talmud explain in great detail how the commandments of the Torah (the first five books of the Bible) are to be carried out. The Talmud is made up of two separate works: the Mishnah, primarily a compilation of Jewish laws, written in Hebrew and edited c. 200 AD in Israel; and the Gemara, c. 500 AD, the rabbinic commentaries and discussions on the Mishnah.

4. **The Sinner's Prayer** is a term that describes the words spoken by a person when he or she acknowledges their sin and their need for a relationship with God through Jesus Christ. There are different versions; this is an example:

> "Father, I know that I have broken Your laws and my sins have separated me from You. I am truly sorry, and now I want to turn away from my past sinful life toward You. Please forgive me, and help me avoid sinning again. I believe that Your son, Jesus Christ, died for my sins, was resurrected from the dead, is alive, and hears my prayer. I invite Jesus to become the Lord of my life, to rule and reign in my heart from this day forward. Please send Your Holy Spirit to help me obey You, and to do Your will for the rest of my life. In Jesus' name I pray, Amen."

5. **Hasidim** are members of a strict form of Orthodox Judaism (Hasidic Jews) founded in Poland in the eighteenth century by Baal Shem-Tov.

6. Jeremiah 31:31–34.

7. Romans 9:25 (see also Hosea 2:23).

8. Psalm 128:3.

9. Psalm 23:6.

10. **Passover Seder** (meaning "order") is a biblical Jewish feast that marks the beginning of the Jewish holiday of Passover (Pesach) which recalls the exodus of the Jewish people from Egypt after generations of slavery. This story is told in Exodus 1 – 15.

11. **Public schools** in America are free to all and are funded by the state. They are not private schools.

12. **New Age movement** (NAM) developed throughout nations in the West during the 1970s. NAM focuses on self-spirituality and healing (particularly using alternative therapies). It draws from both Eastern and Western religious traditions.

13. **The Jesus People** movement started on the West Coast of the United States in the late 1960s and early 1970s and spread rapidly throughout America. It was a counterculture movement that particularly attracted hippies and those seeking a meaningful alternative to the middle class culture of the time.

14. John 3:1–21.

15. 2 Corinthians 3:14.

16. Mark 10:29–30.

17. Matthew 12:48–50.

18. **Aliyah** The immigration of Jewish people to Israel, from nations where they have lived for centuries.

19. Romans 8:28.

20. See note 4.

21. Ephesians 2:15.

22. Ezekiel 20:34.

23. Luke 6:22–23, 26.

24. Romans 1:16.

25. Matthew 10:40.

26. Philippians 2:7.

27. See chapter 1, note1.

28. Psalm 36:1–4, 11–12.

29. **A fatwah** is a ruling on a point of Islamic law given by a recognized authority (Oxford English Dictionary). In this case, an Islamic cleric declared a death sentence.

30. **Intifada**, an uprising; in this case by Palestinians against Israel. The first Palestinian intifada against Israel started in the late 1980s; the second was in the early 2000s.

31. Psalm 23:4.

32. Samuel Marinus Zwemer (1867–1952) was an American missionary who became known as the "Apostle to Islam" for his strenuous, if not always successful, evangelization efforts in Islamic countries. In 1889, along with a colleague, he founded the American Arabian Mission, and the following year he travelled to the Arabian Peninsula. He influenced subsequent generations of missionaries to the Muslim world although he saw only a few Muslims openly profess the Christian faith.

33. The Arabian Peninsula has the largest oil reserves in the world. With the exception of deposits in Yemen, the Arabian oil fields lie in the same great sedimentary basin as the fields of Iran and Iraq. Although oil was discovered in Iran in 1908, the first field on the Arabian side of the basin, in Bahrain, was not found until 1932. This inspired an intensive search in eastern Arabia that in time reached far into the interior. (www.britannica. com)

34. Mark 16:15.

35. Genesis 12:1–3.

36. Zoroaster, founder of Zoroastrianism, the religion of ancient Persia that bears the closest resemblance to Judaism and Christianity. One of the characteristic features of Zoroastrianism is the doctrine of dualism, recognizing the powers of good and evil as two personified principles at war with each other. (www.jewishencyclopedia.com)

37. Romans 11:29.

38. Below is a partial listing of Isaiah's prophecies, based on copyrighted research from the book, *100 Prophecies: Ancient biblical prophecies that foretold the future*, by George Konig and Ray Konig.

Isaiah 7:14 – Isaiah foreshadowed the virgin birth of Jesus.

Isaiah 9:6–7 – There would be a son called God.

Isaiah 13:19 – Babylon's kingdom would be overthrown, permanently.

Isaiah 14:23 – Babylon would be reduced to swampland.

Isaiah 35:4–6 – He would perform miracles.

Isaiah 40:1–5, 9 – The Messiah would be preceded by a messenger.

Isaiah 45:1 – Babylon's gates would open for Cyrus.

Isaiah 49:6 – God's salvation would reach the ends of the earth.

Isaiah 49:13–17 – God will never forget the children of Israel.

Isaiah 50:6 – Jesus was spat upon and beaten.

Isaiah 53:1–3 – The Messiah would be rejected.

Isaiah 53:4–6 – God's servant would die for our sins.

Isaiah 53:7 – God's servant would be silent before his accusers.

Isaiah 53:9 – God's servant would be buried in a rich man's tomb.

Isaiah 53:12 – God's servant would be "numbered with the transgressors".

(www.aboutbibleprophecy.com)

39. "The enemy of my enemy is my friend" is thought to be a quote from an ancient Arabic saying describing how two people who would normally disagree with each other can come together to fight against a shared enemy.

40. During the month of October 1994, all around the world, Christians joined together in "Praying through the Window", probably the most widespread prayer effort in the history of the church. More than 20 million Christians focused on an area called the 10/40 Window. This window stretches across North Africa, through the Middle East and India, on through China, from 10 degrees north of the equator to 40 degrees north. (Mission Frontiers January–February 1994: www.missionfrontiers.org)

41. Matthew 6:14–15.

42. Zechariah 8:22–23.

43. Romans 11:14 (NLT).

44. Ezekiel 36:24–28.

45. The Iraq–Kuwait War started on 2 August 1990, when Saddam Hussein invaded Kuwait.

46. The Jewish diaspora occurred in AD 70 when the Romans sacked Jerusalem and burned down the temple. The Romans renamed Jerusalem Ælia Capitolina, and it became a Roman colony and entirely pagan city. The Jewish population dispersed to many nations including Babylonia, Persia, Spain, France, Germany, Poland, Russia, and the United States. Jewish communities gradually adopted distinctive languages, rituals, and cultures, some assimilating into the countries to which they had travelled more than others. While some lived in peace, others experienced times of severe anti-Semitism.

47. Hosea 3:4–5.

48. Luke 19:41–44.

49. Ezekiel 20:34.

50. Proverbs 24:10–12.

51. The **Six-Day War** in 1967 – also called the June War or Third Arab–Israeli War – took place 5–10 June 1967, and was the third of the Arab–Israeli wars. Israel's decisive victory included the capture of the Sinai Peninsula, Gaza Strip, West Bank, Old City of Jerusalem, and the Golan Heights; the status of these territories subsequently became a major point of contention in the Arab–Israeli conflict. The Arab countries' losses in the conflict were disastrous. Egypt's casualties numbered more than 11,000, with 6,000 for Jordan and 1,000 for Syria, compared with only 700

for Israel. The Arab armies also suffered crippling losses of weaponry and equipment. The lopsidedness of the defeat demoralized both the Arab public and the political elite. Nasser announced his resignation on 9 June but quickly yielded to mass demonstrations calling for him to remain in office. In Israel, which had proved beyond question that it was the region's pre-eminent military power, there was euphoria.

The Six-Day War also marked the start of a new phase in the conflict between Israel and the Palestinians, since the conflict created hundreds of thousands of refugees and brought more than a million Palestinians in the occupied land under Israeli rule. (Encyclopaedia Britannica)

52. The **Church of the Holy Sepulchre** – also known as the **Church of the Resurrection** by Eastern Christians – is a large Christian church that is now situated within the walls of the Old City of Jerusalem, although in Jesus' day this site would have been outside the city walls. The original church was built by Constantine the Great in AD 335, and many consider the site where this church is situated to be Golgotha, where Jesus Christ was crucified. Since the fourth century it has been an important place of pilgrimage for Christians.

53. **Two intifadas** – the first started in December 1987 and the second started in September 2000.

54. **Bir Zeit** is a Palestinian town north of Ramallah in the central West Bank. Its population in the 2007 census was 4,529. Bir Zeit is the home to the Bir Zeit University.

55. The **Coptic Orthodox Church of Alexandria** is the official name for the largest Christian church in Egypt and the Middle East. According to tradition, the church was established by St Mark in the middle of the first century (approximately AD 42). As of 2012, about 10 per cent of Egyptians belonged to the Coptic Orthodox Church of Alexandria.

56. **Moqattam Church, Cairo**:

Hidden in the small streets of the Zabaleen, or the garbage collectors area, at the foot of Moqattam, the Saint Samaan church stands as a testament to the faith of many Egyptians. In 1969 when 15,000 Christian Egyptians collectively left their home villages in Assiut for Cairo to seek work and a better standard of living, the families were given permission by then-president Gamal Abdul-Nasser to live in a deserted area by Moqattam hill. The ramshackle houses turned into the busy area now known as Mansheyet Nasser, or Zabaleen. The families made their living as garbage collectors and made recycling into a profession. To this day every morning piles of trash are dumped in the area by dozens of garbage trucks from all around Cairo and families collect garbage themselves using small donkey carts in the different neighbourhoods of Cairo. Once the garbage is collected it is sorted and recycled. Deep inside the neighbourhood, the Saint Samaan church is carved in the side of the mountain, and is the spiritual heart of the community. Construction of the church started in 1974 by the Egyptian cleric Samaan Ibrahim, going through many phases until reaching its current shape and it has become one of the most significant churches in Egypt. The style of the church exploits the hill's caves and the church's largest hall is an amphitheatre which seats around 10,000 people. The area includes playgrounds for kids, a cafeteria, a library, the administration office and the monastery. The church is open for visitors and tourists and its spectacular location, unique structure and style and the wonderful carvings adorning the hill make it well worth a visit.

(Abdel-Rahman Shereif, *Daily News Egypt*, 14 February 2013)

57. John 3:16.

58. Acts 9.

59. Isaiah 11:11–12.

60. **Jews for Jesus** To quote from their website:

Our name tells who we are, who we stand for and what we do. Everything is right up front! While we might have chosen a less controversial name, Jews for Jesus is the one that most quickly, easily and accurately lets people know who we are and what we are about.

Sometimes people ask us, "How long has Jews for Jesus been around?" We love that question because it gives us the chance to grin and say: "Since AD 32, give or take a year." The joke reminds people that a minority of Jewish people have always believed and proclaimed the gospel, and that we follow in that same tradition.

Actually, Jews for Jesus began as a slogan. In the late 1960s a moving of the Holy Spirit brought thousands of cause-oriented young people to faith in Jesus, many of whom were Jewish. As for our organization, Moishe Rosen officially founded Jews for Jesus in September of 1973. Rosen, a veteran missionary to the Jewish people, was the executive director of the mission for 23 years. He revolutionized evangelistic methods and materials with his creative approach to communicating the gospel, and we believe he was the foremost strategist and tactician in the field of Jewish evangelism.

(www.jewsforjesus.org)

61. **Oral law** – a legal commentary on the Torah, explaining how its commandments are to be carried out in a practical way.

62. **Bar Mitzvah** – literally translates as "son of commandment". The word "bar" means "son" in Aramaic, which was the commonly spoken vernacular language of the Jewish people (and much of the Middle East) from around 500 BC to AD 400. The word "mitzvah" is Hebrew for "commandment". The term "bar mitzvah" refers to two things:

First, when a boy comes of age at 13-years-old he has become a "bar mitzvah" and is recognized by Jewish tradition as having the same rights as a full grown man. A boy who has become a Bar Mitzvah is now morally and ethically responsible for his decisions and actions.

The term "bar mitzvah" also refers to the religious ceremony that accompanies a boy becoming a Bar Mitzvah. Often a celebratory party will follow the ceremony and that party is also called a bar mitzvah.

(www.judaism.about.com)

63. **Tallit** – a Jewish prayer shawl.

64. **Tefillin**:

Tefillin are two small black boxes with black straps attached to them; Jewish men are required to place one box on their head and tie the other one on their arm each weekday morning. *Tefillin* are biblical in origin, and are commanded within the context of several laws outlining a Jew's relationship to God. "And you shall love the Lord your God with all your heart, with all your soul, and with all your might. Take to heart these instructions with which I charge you this day. Impress them upon your children. Recite them when you stay at home and when you are away, when you lie down and when you get up. Bind them as a sign on your hand and let them serve as a frontlet between your eyes" (Deuteronomy 6:5–8).

Tefillin are wrapped around the arm seven times, and the straps on the head are adjusted so they fit snugly.

The text that is inserted inside the two boxes of *Tefillin* is hand-written by a scribe, and consists of the four sets of biblical verses in which *Tefillin* are commanded (Exodus 13:1–10, 11–16; Deuteronomy 6:4–9, 11:13–21). Because each pair of *Tefillin* is hand-written and hand-crafted, it is relatively expensive.

The word *Tefillin* is commonly translated as "phylacteries," though the Hebrew term is more often used.

Putting on *Tefillin* is the first *mitzvah* assumed by a Jewish male upon his Bar Mitzvah. Usually, boys are trained to start wearing them one to two months before their thirteenth Hebrew birthday. During the training period, boys don *Tefillin*, but do not recite a blessing. Subsequent to the Bar Mitzvah, a specific blessing, "Blessed are You, Lord our God, King of the universe, who has sanctified us with His commandments and commanded us to put on *Tefillin*," is recited whenever they are worn. Many Jews say an additional blessing and prayer upon putting on *Tefillin*.

Tefillin are worn each weekday morning, but not on the Sabbath or on most Jewish holidays. On the fast day of Tisha Be'Av, and on that day only, they are put on during the afternoon instead of the morning service.

(From www.jewishvirtuallibrary.org/jsource/Judaism/tefillin.html)

65. **Adonai Roi** – Messianic congregation in Tel Aviv. (www.adonairoi.com)

66. Biblical prophecies regarding the return of the Jewish people to live in Israel include:

Zechariah 8:7–8.

Isaiah 43:5–6.

Isaiah 11:10–12.

Jeremiah 30:3–4.

67   Jeremiah 30:22.

68   Luke 13:34.

69. Luke 13:35.

70. Isaiah 43:5–6.

71. Ezekiel 37:1–14.

72. Isaiah 49:6.

73. Romans 10:2.

74. Zechariah 8:23.

75. John 17:20–21.

76. John 15:16.

77. John 15:5.

78. John 8:36.

79. Jeremiah 19:15.

80. 1 Peter 5:8.

81. **Chuppah** – a canopy or covering that is attached to the tops of four poles, under which a couple stand during their Jewish wedding ceremony. The word "chuppah" means covering or protection, and is intended as a roof or covering for the bride and groom at their wedding.

82. Ephesians 2:14–16.

83. Joel 2:25.

84. Zechariah 12:10.